EARTH & SKY

DOVER PUBLICATIONS, INC.
MINEOLA, NEW YORK

Bibliographical Note

Earth & Sky, first published by Dover Publications, Inc., in 2015, contains pages from the following online workbooks published by Education.com: *Why is the Sky Blue?, Energy All Around, Landforms for Kids,* and *Geography Math.*

International Standard Book Number

ISBN-13: 978-0-486-80269-5
ISBN-10: 0-486-80269-8

Manufactured in the United States by Courier Corporation
80269801   2015
www.doverpublications.com

CONTENTS

Contents

WHY IS THE SKY BLUE?

Why is the sky blue?

To understand why the sky is blue, we must first understand the physics of light and color.

The light from the sun seems white to us, but white light is actually made up of all the colors of the spectrum: red, orange, yellow, green, blue, indigo and violet!

We see objects in color because those objects absorb some of the colors in white light, and reflect the colors that we see! For example, grass reflects the color green and absorbs all the other colors.

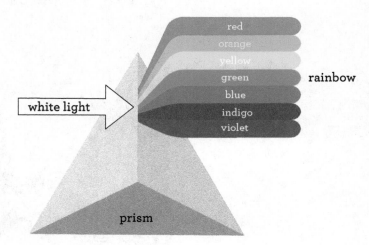

white light

red
orange
yellow
green
blue
indigo
violet

rainbow

prism

The sky is blue because it has to travel through Earth's atmosphere, where there are lots of gases that absorb red, orange and yellow colors. Then, the blue light gets scattered all across the sky, which is what we see when we look into the sky.

QUESTION & ANSWER:

What colors make up the white light of the sun?

....

....

If you see a blue car, what color/s does it reflect?

....

....

If you see a red apple, what color/s does it absorb?

....

....

Why is the ocean blue?

The ocean appears blue to us because of the light from the sun.

We often think that the sun's light just allows us to see, but without light, colors wouldn't even exist!

What we see as white light from the sun is actually a combination of all the colors of the rainbow. Try and imagine red, orange, yellow, green, blue, indigo and violet rays of light streaming from the sun. Objects either absorb or reflect these rays.

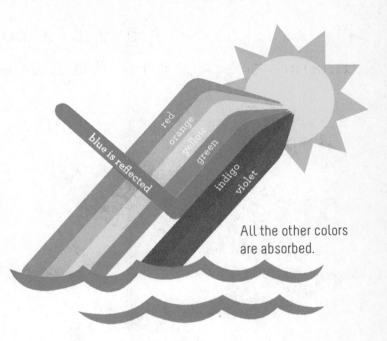

All the other colors are absorbed.

QUESTION & ANSWER:

What colors make up the light from the sun?

....

....

What color/s does the ocean reflect?

....

....

What color/s does the ocean absorb?

....

....

When the sun's light hits the ocean, the red, orange, yellow, green, indigo and violet rays are absorbed so that we can't see them! Only the blue light is reflected. The ocean itself isn't really blue; we're just seeing the reflected blue light.

Why is the ocean salty?

The ocean has been salty for a long time–way before humans were around to use it as a seasoning!

Millions of years ago when our planet was first forming, gasses from deep within the earth started bubbling up to the surface. These gasses contained tons of salt, and when they bubbled up into the ocean, the salt was released.

Today, rain water continues to deposit even more salt into the ocean. When rain droplets fall on land, they often pick up pieces of salt. Some of these droplets slip and slide across the land to eventually reach the ocean.

ACTIVITY:

Make your own salt water by mixing several teaspoonfuls of regular table salt into a glass of water. Leave it out on a sunny windowsill for a couple of days. The water will evaporate, but salt residue will stay in the glass.

Why do you think this happens?

Why do we yawn?

We often yawn because we are sleepy or bored. Sometimes we even yawn because someone next to us yawned.

Scientists have a lot of theories to explain why these situations cause us to yawn, but nobody knows exactly why it happens. One theory is that our bodies are trying to get more oxygen.

That's why we take a yawn, which is essentially just a bigger breath than usual. Another theory states that our bodies are trying to cool our brains by taking in more air.

ACTIVITY:

Did you know that the average adult yawns 20 times per day? Ask the members of your family to keep track of their yawns for one whole day. Graph the results here.

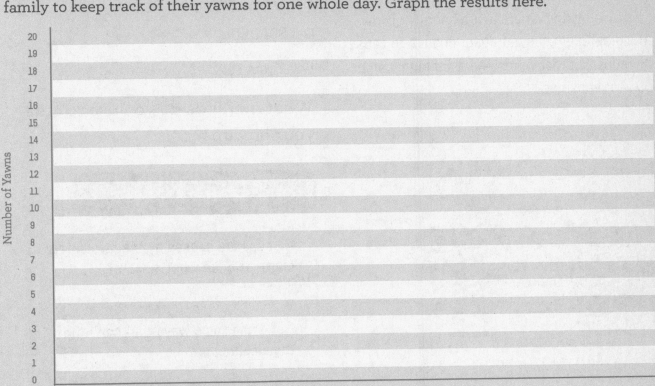

Number of Yawns

Family Members

Why do we hiccup?

The often annoying hiccup happens when our diaphragms get upset.

The diaphragm is a muscle at the bottom of the rib cage that helps pull air into our lungs when we breathe. Every once in a while, the diaphragm gets irritated and starts pulling air into the lungs the wrong way. We experience this as a hiccup.

Eating too quickly, drinking cold beverages, and swallowing air are just a handful of ways the diaphragm can get upset enough to cause hiccups. In other words, the diaphragm can be kind of sensitive.

There are lots of "home remedies" that people use to get rid of the hiccups. Lots of them are silly.

Do you think any of these methods actually work? Why or why not?

Eat a spoonful of sugar.

Drink water from the opposite side of the glass.

Chug a glass of water.

Hold your breath.

Get SCARED!

Cover your ears.

What methods do you use to cure your hiccups?

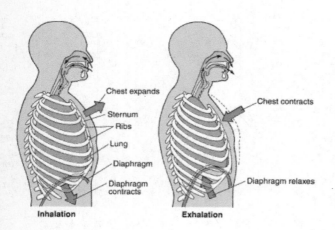

Chest expands
Sternum
Ribs
Lung
Diaphragm
Diaphragm contracts
Inhalation

Chest contracts
Diaphragm relaxes
Exhalation

QUESTION & ANSWER:

Hiccups are caused by the involuntary contraction of what muscle?

. . . .

List down some ways that can irritate the diaphragm.

. . . .

. . . .

Why do people blush?

When some people get embarrassed, their cheeks turn red. We call this blushing, and it also can occur when a person is anxious or angry.

The science behind blushing is pretty simple: your body sends extra blood to your face which causes your cheeks to redden. The reason this happens is not so clear. Scientists have suggested that our bodies blush to reveal how we really feel. Next time you're anxious to get in a game or embarrassed that you dropped your ice cream on the floor, your cheeks just might give you away!

Did you know that some people are afraid of blushing? The fear of blushing is called erythrophobia.

Why do you think people suffer from erythrophobia?

QUESTION & ANSWER:

What causes your cheeks to redden?

. . . .

. . . .

What is a possible reason behind blushing?

. . . .

. . . .

What is erythrophobia?

. . . .

. . . .

Why do we dream?

In our dreams, we can be anything from superheroes to animal tamers, but we can also be pursued by monsters or arrive late to school. But why do we have certain dreams? Do our dreams mean anything? Scientists have lots of theories to answer these questions, but no real answers quite yet.

Dreaming may be our bodies' way of storing up memories and thoughts. Throughout the day, we each create a nearly infinite amount of experiences. These experiences may organize themselves in our brains as dreams.

Another theory is that dreams help our bodies interpret what our brains have been thinking about. If you dream about missing the bus and forgetting all your school supplies, you may be nervous about school starting.

Zzzzz....

ACTIVITY:

We remember our dreams best immediately after we wake up. Keep a notepad by your bed tonight and write down everything you remember tomorrow morning.

Can you figure out why you dreamed what you did?

Why do cats purr?

Cats purr for the same reason that humans sigh, smile and sing. It's a communication tool that means different things at different times.

A cat's purr can be broken down into three separate categories: the happy purr, the friendly purr and the reassuring purr.

The happy purr is the most popular purr. When you scratch a cat behind the ears, the purr signals the cat's own comfort and enjoyment. The friendly purr often happens when a cat is approached by a human he likes or another cat. This second type of purr simply communicates that the cat welcomes the visitor. Lastly, cats use the reassuring purr when they are afraid. Scientists believe that purring calms the cat, in the same way humans sometimes sing when they're nervous to make them feel better.

Identification:

Based on the reading, identify what type of purr cats make in these situations:

. . . . a cat being scratched

. . . . two cats walking towards each other

. . . . a cat at a vet

. . . . when a cat gets a treat

. . . . a mother cat giving birth

. . . . when approached by a stranger

Mechanics behind a purr:

Purrs involve various muscles in a cat's body. The larynx, or voice box, and diaphragm play key roles in the mechanics of purring.

vocal cords

The diaphragm moves the air in and out of the vibrating vocal cords which causes the sound.

Why does ice float?

Even though ice is the solid form of water, it actually has a lower density than its liquid counterpart.

When water freezes, its molecules actually spread out a bit and organize themselves into crystal arrangements. Water molecules, on the other hand, have tightly packed molecules. So when you put an ice cube into a glass of water, the ice cannot sink to the bottom of the glass because the molecules in the water are too dense.

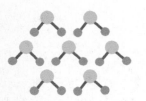

ice molecules

cold water molecules

ACTIVITY:

Try your own experiment. You know that ice cubes float in water, but what about other liquids? Record your findings here.

....

....

....

....

....

....

....

Why does hair turn gray?

To find out why hair turns gray we have to investigate *hair follicles*.

Hair follicles are tubes of tissue that surround the roots of each hair strand. Inside the hair follicles are *pigment cells* that determine if our hair is red, brown, black or blond. As people age, their hair follicles start to die. Without enough pigment cells from these dying hair follicles, hair gradually turns gray or white.

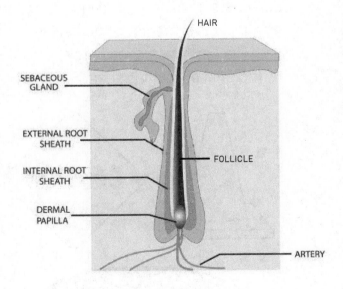

HAIR

SEBACEOUS GLAND

EXTERNAL ROOT SHEATH

INTERNAL ROOT SHEATH

DERMAL PAPILLA

FOLLICLE

ARTERY

QUESTION & ANSWER:

What are the tubes of tissue that surround the roots of each hair strand?

. . . .

. . . .

Located inside the hair follicles, what determines the color of our hair?

. . . .

. . . .

What helps determine whether a person's hair turns gray or white?

. . . .

. . . .

There isn't a certain age when every person starts getting gray hair. It depends on each individual's *genes*. A good way to predict when or if someone you know might get gray hair is to look at that person's parents or grandparents.

Why are manhole covers round?

Manhole covers are removable metal plates that cover manholes. They have been around at least since ancient Rome, where there were stone sewer grates.

They are round for several different reasons. The round shape is easiest to roll when workers need to maneuver the covers out of the way. Workers don't have to rotate the cover in a certain way to fit it back in the hole. You can also get scientific about manhole covers. A round manhole cannot fall into the circular hole it covers, but any other shape could if it were to fall in diagonally.

TRIVIA:

Did you know that big companies like Microsoft and Google used to ask potential employees why manhole covers are round?

Why do you think technological companies would ask this during a job interview?

What would your answer be?

Scientists also say that round manhole covers resist compression from the Earth's crust and prevent traffic from dislodging them.

Why does the earth spin?

The Earth spins because there is nothing in its way to stop it!

Long before our planet was a solid sphere, there was just a mass of dust and gas. Earth was formed when all this matter began to spin. That's how most planets and stars are formed!

Thousands of years later, the spinning cloud of dust and gas became our planet, and thanks to our position in the Solar System, neither the sun nor the moon had the power to slow Earth's rotation enough to halt it completely.

QUESTION & ANSWER:

What was Earth before it became a solid sphere?

....

....

How was Earth formed?

....

....

Can the sun and the moon stop Earth from spinning?

....

....

Imagine the Earth did not spin. How would this affect your life?

⭐ Remember that the Earth's rotation is responsible for the sun rising and setting. If the Earth did not spin, parts of our planet would spend half a year in darkness and another half a year in full sunlight.

Why is there a leap year?

The month of February usually has 28 days, but every four years it has 29. To understand this we have to understand what a year is.

One year is supposed to match the time it takes for the Earth to orbit the Sun. However, the match isn't perfect. Our year equals 365 days, but it takes Earth about 365 ¼ days to complete its orbit. That little fraction may seem insignificant, but every four years it adds up to a complete day. We give that extra day to February and call it leap year.

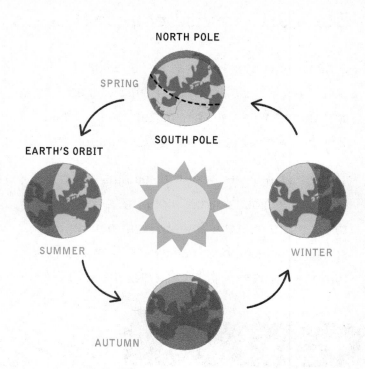

NORTH POLE

SPRING

SOUTH POLE

EARTH'S ORBIT

WINTER

SUMMER

AUTUMN

QUESTION & ANSWER:

How long does it take the Earth to complete its orbit?

. . . .

How often does a leap year occur?

. . . .

What is a person born on February 29th called?

. . . .

A leap year consists of how many days?

. . . .

Why is it called leap year when we're actually adding a day? It seems like it might make more sense to call it some thing like plus day or add day. We call it leap year because the addition of that one day effectively leaps the rest of that year forward by 24 hours.

A "leap year baby" is someone who is born on the last day of February in a leap year. Would a leap year baby age differently than everyone else?

How is honey made?

Without bees we wouldn't have any delicious honey to sweeten our toast or tea. Honey bees work tirelessly to produce honey in a multi-step process that is both wonderful and a bit disgusting.

First, honey bees have to use their tongues to slurp out the pollen and nectar from flowers. They actually digest all of this, allowing the pollen and nectar to mix with the proteins and enzymes of their stomachs. When the honey bees return to their hive, they regurgitate—a fancy word for throwing up this pollen/nectar/protein /enzyme mix into a beeswax comb.

The bees then flap their wings to help the mixture thicken before covering the combs with a wax cap.

After beekeepers take out these honeycombs, all they need to do is process and clean out the combs a bit. The odd combination of flower parts and bee proteins is now honey!

Can you help our bee friend find his mate?

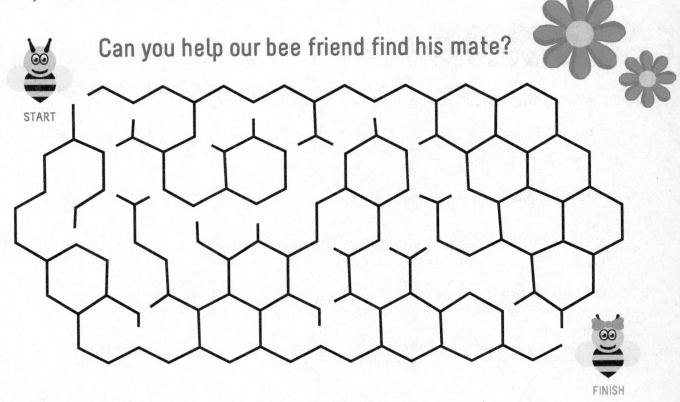

START

FINISH

How is a pearl formed?

Have you ever had a small piece of dust get in your eye? It was probably annoying, but when an oyster gets dust inside its shell, it turns the dust speck into a pearl!

Oysters try and protect themselves from unwanted visitors by covering any outside dust particles with a mineral substance called nacre. Layers and layers of nacre eventually form a pearl.

Natural pearls form when a piece of dust gets into an oyster's shell by chance. Cultured pearls are the result of humans forcing a dust particle into an oyster's shell. Pearls are so popular today that a lot of people don't want to wait for a pearl to form naturally!

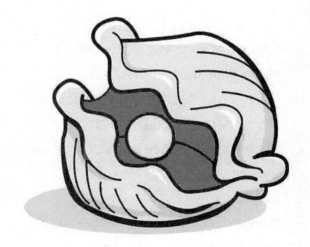

QUESTION & ANSWER:

How do oysters protect themselves?

....

....

How do natural pearls form?

....

....

How do cultured pearls form?

....

....

Can you think of anything else in nature that starts off small? and plain, but after a long time turns into something beautiful?

How is a star born?

A star is a big ball of plasma that is formed from a cloud of dust and gas.

Sometimes particles of dust and gas float by each other in space without anything happening. Other times gravity clumps these clouds together into compact substances. The particles begin bouncing off of each other, creating friction and heat. Eventually, the heat becomes so intense that it creates a nuclear reaction which releases a massive amount of energy and light. The resulting substance is a star.

QUESTION & ANSWER:

What is a star?

....

....

What gets released after a nuclear reaction involving intense heat?

....

....

Did you know that celebrities and actors are often called stars?

Why do you think we compare famous people to burning lights in the sky?

Why does it rain?

Rain comes from clouds, which are themselves made up of lots and lots of tiny droplets of water that are holding on to each other.

When the sun shines on the earth, it causes water to evaporate. The water can come from lakes, oceans, seas and even from your pool outside. As this water evaporates it rises to the atmosphere. When it reaches an altitude (height) where the temperature is very low, it condenses to form clouds. When heavy enough, these clouds release water droplets which fall back to the earth as rain or hail.

Experiment:

Note: Ask an adult to help you with this activity

What You Need:
saucepan   ice cubes
water   oven mitt

Directions:
1. Ask an adult to boil some water in a saucepan.
2. Using oven mitts to protect your hands, hold a tray of ice above the steam.
3. Drops will begin to fall like rain from the tray.

Why does this happen?
The cold surface of the ice cube tray cools the steam from the boiling water, changing it back into water in the form of rain drops.

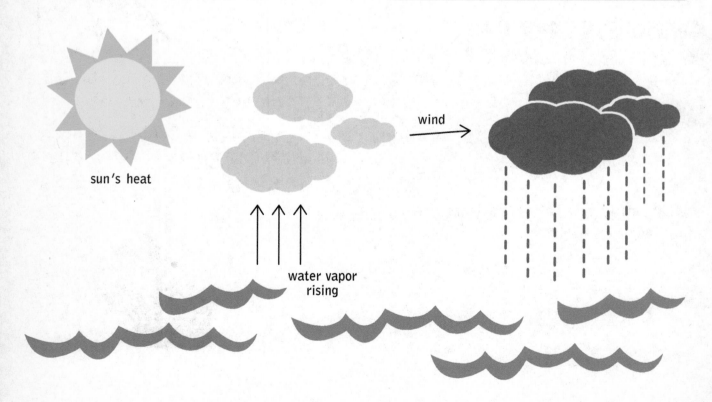

sun's heat

wind

water vapor rising

Great job!

_____

is an Education.com science superstar

ENERGY ALL AROUND

WHAT IS ENERGY?

Energy is defined as the ability to do work. There is energy in everything, and we use energy for everything we do.

There are 2 types of energy: **potential and kinetic.**

POTENTIAL ENERGY IS ENERGY THAT IS STORED.

A car sitting at the top of a hill has potential energy.

KINETIC ENERGY IS ENERGY THAT IS IN MOTION.

When the car begins to go down the hill, the potential energy has turned into kinetic energy.

POTENTIAL VERSUS KINETIC ENERGY

Take a look at the chart to see some examples of potential and kinetic energy.

POTENTIAL ENERGY	KINETIC ENERGY
A car sitting in the driveway	A car driving down the street
A ball in a basketball player's hands	A ball bouncing down the court
A sleeping child	A child jumping on the bed
A log in a fireplace	A burning log
A lamp	A lamp turned on

Look at the pictures below, and label them potential or kinetic based on what type of energy they are showing.

DIFFERENT FORMS OF ENERGY

Energy comes in different forms, and each can be changed into another form.

HERE ARE SIX DIFFERENT FORMS OF ENERGY

CHEMICAL ENERGY

is the energy stored within bonds between molecules. There are many sources for this energy, such as natural gas, gasoline and coal.

THERMAL ENERGY

(or heat energy) is the energy of moving molecules. The energy that comes from a fire is thermal energy.

MECHANICAL ENERGY

is the energy stored in objects by tension. When the tension is released, motion occurs. A spring that is pressed down has mechanical energy.

RADIANT ENERGY

(or light energy) is related to the movement of light. The Sun provides radiant energy to warm our planet.

ELECTRICAL ENERGY

is energy that comes from tiny charged particles called electrons. In nature, lightning is one form of electrical energy.

NUCLEAR ENERGY

is the energy created when the nuclei of atoms are split or fused. This type of energy is produced in nuclear power plants.

ENERGY IS ALL AROUND US

Humans have always depended on energy for many things. From basic survival, such as cooking food, to the luxuries of television and video games, energy is an important part of our daily lives.

Before electricity, humans had to rely on the other sources of energy found in nature to complete tasks.

ACTIVITY

Look at the pictures below and label what form of energy is being used.

1

_____

2

_____

3

_____

4

_____

Think about the first two images above and write about what electrical devices help us to do these tasks today.

RENEWABLE VERSUS
NON-RENEWABLE ENERGY

Energy is all around us in nature. Some sources of energy will never run out so that energy is known as renewable energy. Other sources of energy are available in specific amounts and will not regenerate, so they make non-renewable energy; it is energy from a source that will run out.

BIOMASS, WIND, WATER, GEOTHERMAL, SOLAR

Efforts are being made today to use more of these energy sources which are sometimes called "green energy" sources.

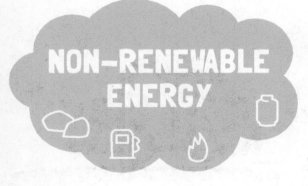

COAL, NATURAL GAS, PETROLEUM (OR CRUDE OIL), PROPANE, URANIUM

Coal, petroleum, natural gas and propane are known as fossil fuels because of the way they were formed.

WHAT IS BIOMASS ENERGY?

Biomass fuels come from living things such as trees, plants and crop residue. As long as we continue to grow trees and plants and replace those we use by planting new ones, we will always have biomass fuels.

TAKE A LOOK AT HOW BIOMASS ENERGY IS PRODUCED.

1 The original source of biomass fuels is from the sun. The energy is stored in trees and plants.

2 When trees or plants die or are cut down, they are burned.

steam

3 Steam is released and moves blades inside a turbine or generator.

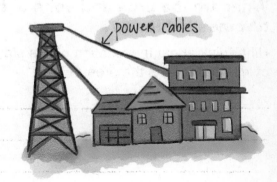

power cables

4 The power is then transferred to homes and businesses via cables.

★ THINK AND RESPOND ★

1. List 5 reasons why people cut down trees.

_____

2. Why is it important that we plant new trees?

_____

27

WHAT IS WIND ENERGY?

Wind is caused by convection currents (flow of air) in Earth's atmosphere. The sun produces the heat energy that produces these currents. The wind is full of kinetic energy.

Wind can be transferred into electrical energy with the help of wind turbines. A **turbine** is a machine powered by rotating blades.

The blades of a wind turbine move when there is wind. The energy is then transferred to a generator by a spinning shaft.

Windmills work the same as turbines. They are used for grinding grains or pumping water. These have been used around the world for over 1,000 years.

Wind must be blowing at a rate of at least 14 miles per hour to power a turbine or windmill. Very strong winds, however, can damage these structures.

THINK AND RESPOND

What are the pros and cons of building wind turbines in Florida?

Hint: Think about the location of this state and what type of weather affects the area.

_____

_____

_____

_____

_____

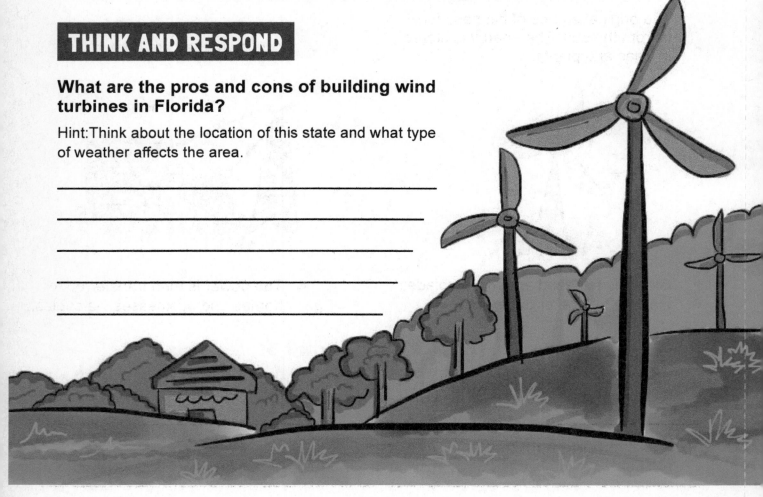

WHAT IS WATER ENERGY?

Water energy, also known as hydro power, is generated by moving water. The kinetic energy in moving water can be transferred into electicity. Here's how electricity is made at a hydroelectric power plant.

STEP 1

A dam is built to collect water (usually on a large river).

STEP 2

A gate is opened in the dam to allow water to rush into a large pipe. The pipe is sloped so that the water moves quickly, creating large amounts of kinectic energy.

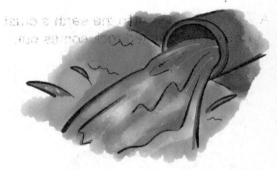

STEP 3

The rushing water moves the blades, which in turn sends power to a generator.

generator

★ THINK AND RESPOND ★

Could a hydroelectric power plant be built on a lake? Explain why or why not.

_____

_____

WHAT IS GEOTHERMAL ENERGY?

Geothermal energy is produced by hot rocks underground. To harness this energy, deep wells are drilled into the earth. Then, cold water is pumped down into these wells. When the water goes through cracks in the rock, it is heated up. Upon its return to the surface, it has transformed into steam and hot water. This energy is then used to power generators.

Most places on the planet where geothermal energy is found are not visible. However, there are some places where geothermal energy makes its way to the surface. These places are volcanoes, fumaroles, hot springs and geysers.

A **VOLCANO** is a vent in the earth's crust in which hot, melted rock comes out.

A **FUMAROLE** is a hole in the ground where vapors and gas come out. These are usually found in volcanic regions.

A **HOT SPRING** is a source of water which flows out at a temperature higher than the average temperature of other springs.

A **GEYSER** is a spring that occasionally shoots out hot water and steam.

Using the vocabulary above (words in purple), complete the following sentences.

1. There is a _____ in Yellowstone National Park named Old Faithful that shoots out hot water like clockwork every day.

2. When a _____ is erupting, it is a good idea to get out of its path.

3. Many people take advantage of the warm waters of a _____.

4. The steam coming out of a _____ looks a lot like smoke.

WHAT IS SOLAR ENERGY?

Solar energy comes from the sun. The sun is an important resource, as it helps sustain life. Without the sun, our planet would have no life. Through the use of technology, we are able to harness the energy from the sun to convert it to electricity.

SOLAR CELLS are tools that change light energy from the sun and other light sources into electricity. Many calculators use solar cells to power them.

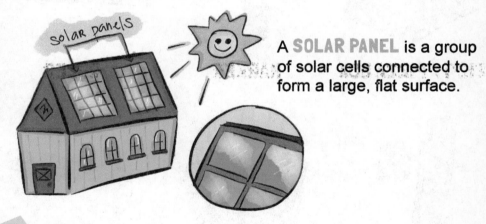

solar panels

A **SOLAR PANEL** is a group of solar cells connected to form a large, flat surface.

THINK AND DRAW

What do you think a car powered by the sun would look like? Draw a picture.

MAKE A SOLAR OVEN

In this fun project, you will harness the power and heat of the sun to cook a cheese quesadilla!

To complete this project, you will need the following materials, as well as an adult to assist you:

EMPTY PIZZA BOX   **MARKER**   **RULER**   **SCISSORS**

GLUE STICK   **BLACK CONSTRUCTION PAPER**   **ALUMINUM FOIL**   **CRAFT KNIFE**

⚠ to be used by an adult

BAMBOO SKEWER, STICK OR DOWEL   **CLEAR PLASTIC WRAP**   **FLOUR TORTILLA**   **CHEESE**

1. Using your ruler and a pencil, measure a window with a 1 inch margin on each side of the top of the box.

2. Have an adult cut three sides with a craft knife, leaving one edge connected.

3. Carefully pry open the flap. This will become your sun window. Fold the window up along the uncut line.

4. Glue the aluminum foil to the inside of your window, smoothing out as many wrinkles as possible.

5. Line the rest of the box with foil, inside and out.

6. Tape the black piece of construction paper on the inside bottom of the box, on top of the foil.

7. Glue the plastic wrap to the underside of the lid. Try to make the seal as airtight as possible.

8. Place a flour tortilla on a piece of aluminum foil and cover half of the torilla with cheese.

9. Put the prepared tortilla (with foil underneath) into your oven and place outside in the sun.

10. Close the box.

11. Use a bamboo skewer, stick or dowel to prop the flap open.

12. Choose an angle that reflects the most light into the solar oven.

13. Cook! Check your food every 10 minutes. This could take anywhere from 20 minutes to 2 hours depending on how sunny it is outside.

14. When the cheese is melted, fold the tortilla in half and enjoy!

RENEWABLE ENERGY
review

ANSWER THE FOLLOWING QUESTIONS ABOUT RENEWABLE ENERGY.

1. Why is it important to try to use as many renewable resources as possible?

2. Name all 5 renewable energy sources and give a brief description of each.

LOOK AT THE FOLLOWING PICTURES AND LABEL THEM ACCORDING TO WHICH RENEWABLE ENERGY SOURCE THEY DEMONSTRATE.

NON- RENEWABLE ENERGY

FOSSIL FUELS

Most non-renewable energy is generated from fossil fuels which include coal, petroleum (crude oil) and natural gas. These are known as fossil fuels because of the way they are formed.

Fossil fuels were formed deep within the Earth from the remains of ancient animals and plants. Over a long period of time, heat and pressure turned these remains into fuel which releases energy when it is burned. Because they take millions of years to form, these fuels are considered non-renewable. If we run out of these, we will have to turn to alternative sources of energy.

COMPARE Using the Venn diagram, compare fossil fuels to solar energy.

FOSSIL FUELS   SOLAR ENERGY

CONSERVING ENERGY ♻

No matter which source of energy you are using, it's important that we don't waste energy. To **conserve** means to not waste or overuse something. Conserving energy is an important part of protecting our environment. Turning off electronic devices when they are not being used, or riding your bike down the street instead of having your mom drive you in a car are two simple ways to conserve energy.

THINK AND RESPOND

Make a list of 5 things you can do to conserve energy.

1 _____
_____

2 _____
_____

3 _____
_____

4 _____
_____

5 _____
_____

VOCABULARY REVIEW

ENERGY   POTENTIAL   KINETIC   RENEWABLE   NON-RENEWABLE   BIOMASS
VOLCANO   FUMAROLE   GEYSER   HOT SPRING   SOLAR CELL   SOLAR PANEL
TURBINE   CONSERVE   Tip: → ↓ ← ↗ ↘ ↙ ↖

```
P V B I O M A S S C A G Q U U T O E P F
D O G X X P R E O J H U E U U Q L I A O
R L Z X G W O N L S R M W Y Y B Q H R T
T C W S R P S T O O M E D I A X C O J R
U A T A O E U L E R R K S W G F O T E C
R N S W R E A E A N T A E Y L J I S N J
B O Z V I R N R N N T N M U E S G P E M
I G E O C I L I M I E I M U N G L R R S
N P A E B G G M X R V A A O F E M I G G
E T L R S O L A R P A N E L O P S N Y U
N O N R E N E W A B L E M N O N Z G O D
L L E C R A L O S G W K I N E T I C L B
```

- Energy in motion is called_____ energy.
- Stored energy is called _____ energy.
- A machine powered by rotating blades is a _____.
- A spring that shoots out hot water is a _____.
- Sources of energy that will never run out are known as _____energy.
- Energy that comes from things such as plants and trees is known as _____ energy.
- _____ is the ability to do work.
- A hole in the ground that has vapors or gases coming out is called a _____.
- A tool that changes light energy into electricity is a _____.
- _____ means to use something in small amounts.
- A _____ is a vent in the Earth's crust in which melted rock comes out.
- Energy available in a specific amount that will not regenerate is known as: _____ _____ energy.
- A _____ is a group of solar cells connected to form a large, flat surface.
- A source of warm water is called a _____.

Great job!

is an Education.com science superstar

LANDFORMS FOR KIDS

What is a landform?

A **landform** is any natural feature of Earth's surface that is made up of rock, dirt or minerals. Landforms can be created in many different ways, including through weathering and erosion, by volcanic eruptions, by the movement of Earth's crust and can even be affected by the growth of living things!

Landforms Wordsearch

```
K C A N Y O N L B P M E S A
M P N B P C T A E U U H E U
R O D P L A T E A U T T T Y
H R U D L V P K A R S T K A
I U V N E E A T J R H O E R
V I A K T T K C L I F F A D
A S L E H A E I K I E D T A
L H C T I M I H A C T U X N
L A A U F A G N U R R N L G
E I P O A D E J R B I E W O
Y P E N I N S U L A S O Y F
S J A F A R A S E U H I L L
```

Find the following landform terms in the wordsearch above.

Karst	Mountain	Plateau	Peninsula
Cave	Yardang	Canyon	Cape
Valley	Butte	Cliff	
Hill	Mesa	Dune	

What is the rock cycle?

The **rock cycle** is a gradual process of movement and change that constantly reshapes our landscape. Processes on and within Earth—including weather, pressure and temperature—cause rocks to break down, melt and solidify over and over. Rocks change from one form to another, but are never destroyed.

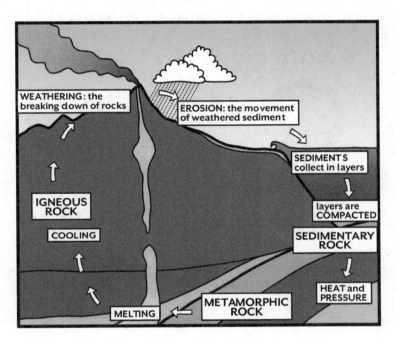

WEATHERING: the breaking down of rocks

EROSION: the movement of weathered sediment

SEDIMENTS collect in layers

layers are COMPACTED

IGNEOUS ROCK

COOLING

SEDIMENTARY ROCK

HEAT and PRESSURE

METAMORPHIC ROCK

MELTING

The Three Types of Rock:

Sedimentary rocks are made from layers of sediment.

Metamorphic rocks are formed under extreme heat and pressure.

Igneous rocks are melted rock that has cooled and hardened.

Processes within the earth push rocks up to the surface, where they're broken down and moved through **weathering** and **erosion**. Bits of rock and sand called **sediment** are deposited in layers. Pressure squeezes the layers and they solidify to form **sedimentary rock**. These rocks gradually move deeper underground, where they encounter extreme heat and pressure that transforms them into **metamorphic rock**. Rocks that are pushed even deeper toward the intense heat of Earth's mantle will melt and become magma. Magma that reaches Earth's surface cools and hardens to form **igneous rock**. This constant recycling of rock has occurred for millions of years, which means that some rocks have been around since the time of the dinosaurs!

What is weathering?

Weathering is the gradual breaking down of rocks and minerals on Earth's surface. There are two main types of weathering: physical and chemical. Physical weathering includes pressure, water and temperature changes. Chemical weathering includes oxidation, biological action and dissolution (the dissolving of certain kinds of rocks).

Chemical Weathering

Physical Weathering

Dissolution contributes to the formation of many caves.

Temperature changes can cause weathering on mountains and rock formations.

Weathering by water contributes to the formation of canyons and valleys.

What is erosion?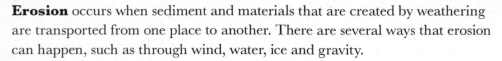

Erosion occurs when sediment and materials that are created by weathering are transported from one place to another. There are several ways that erosion can happen, such as through wind, water, ice and gravity.

Erosion

Wind and water both erode material from canyons.

Wind both builds and moves sand dunes in the desert.

Water moves sediment downstream through valleys to the ocean.

Both gravity and glaciers transport materials from mountains.

Continents

A **continent** is a large land mass, larger than an island, that is partly or completely separated from other land masses by water. There are 7 continents on Earth.

Continental Match-up!

Unscramble the continents' names below. Then the number from the map in the box next to the name.

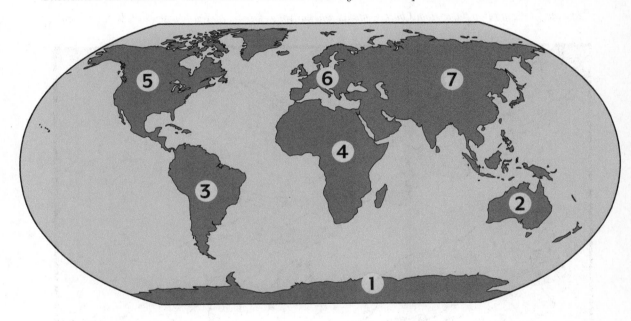

☐ **AASI** _ _ _ _

☐ **RIAFAC** _ _ _ _ _ _

☐ **ICARTACTAN** _ _ _ _ _ _ _ _ _ _

☐ **TRONH REICAMA** _ _ _ _ _ _ _ _ _ _ _ _

☐ **REOPEU** _ _ _ _ _ _

☐ **SHOUT CERIAAM** _ _ _ _ _ _ _ _ _ _ _ _

☐ **STAIURALA** _ _ _ _ _ _ _ _ _

Plateaus

A **plateau** is a large, flat area of land that is raised higher than the surrounding land. They are usually caused by uplift through tectonic action, and then are worn down by wind and water, forming canyons, mesas, buttes and other formations.

Landscape Labeling!

Read the following two pages about buttes, mesas and canyons. Use what you learned to label this landscape.

1) _____

2) _____

3) _____

4) _____

 Did you know? *The layers of rock seen in the walls of the Grand Canyon, located on the Colorado Plateau, were deposited over millions of years. Erosion and weathering from the Colorado River have exposed these ancient rock layers. The bottom of the canyon contains the oldest layers: the Vishnu, Brahma, and Rama Schists. These layers were formed between 1.73 and 1.75 billion years ago, during the Precambrian period!*

Buttes

A **butte** is a tall, steep-sided hill, with a top that is narrower than its height. Buttes look like rock towers.

West Mitten Butte in Monument Valley, located on the border of Arizona and Utah, got its name from its unique shape, which looks just like a mitten. In fact, there is a matching East Mitten Butte nearby, making a pair!

Mesas

A **mesa** is a steep sided hill with a flat top that is wider than it is tall. *Mesa* is Spanish for table, so these features are sometimes nicknamed "table tops."

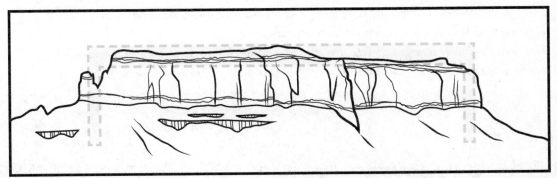

Sentinel Mesa in Monument Valley is a good example of a mesa, because you can clearly see the table shape.

Canyons

A **canyon** is similar to a narrow valley with very steep sides that is carved by a river. **Cliffs**, which are steep rock faces, are common in canyons.

WORD BANK:

COLCA	TAROKO	FISH RIVER
SAMARIA	KINGS	WAIMEA
COPPER	GRAND	ANTELOPE
TIGER LEAPING	TODRA	VERDON

ACROSS:

1) This immense canyon is located in Namibia, Africa.

3) This canyon in Peru is twice as deep as the Grand Canyon.

5) This colorful canyon is on the beautiful island of Kauai.

7) This canyon, located in Arizona, has the same name as an animal.

9) This canyon is located in the Atlas Mountains of Morocco.

11) This canyon in Australia has a very royal sounding name.

13) The Colorado River runs through this amazing canyon in Arizona.

DOWN:

2) This canyon, located on the island of Crete, contains forests of cypress and pine trees.

4) This canyon is located in China, and is a contender for the deepest canyon in the world.

6) This canyon in Mexico shares a name with a common metal.

8) This canyon in France is named after the river that flows through it, and its turquoise-green waters.

9) The name of this canyon in Taiwan means "magnificent and beautiful" in a local language.

1 ACROSS: F I S H R I V E R

Yardangs

Yardangs are rock formations that are mostly found in very dry deserts. They are formed by steady wind erosion, and they often resemble the bows of overturned ships sticking out of the ground.

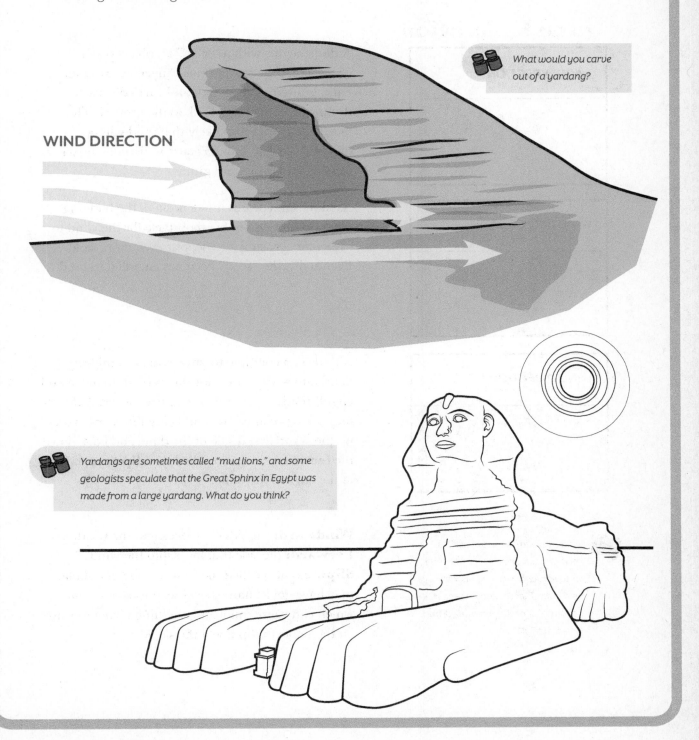

What would you carve out of a yardang?

WIND DIRECTION

Yardangs are sometimes called "mud lions," and some geologists speculate that the Great Sphinx in Egypt was made from a large yardang. What do you think?

Dunes

A **dune** is a hill of sand that has been built up by the wind or by water. Dunes can come in many different shapes and sizes, and are found mostly in arid deserts or near sandy beaches.

Dune Formation

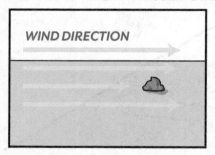

WIND DIRECTION

A dune begins with a "seed," an object on the ground that the sand grains can collect around. Sand is lifted by the wind, and carried a short distance before falling back to the ground. The "seed" makes it more likely that sand will be deposited in that spot, because it disrupts the wind, causing it to drop sand grains.

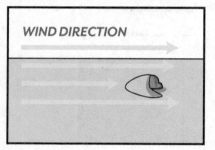

WIND DIRECTION

As more sand grains are deposited, the budding dune becomes more of an obstacle for the wind to overcome, causing it to deposit even more sand. Eventually, the "seed" becomes engulfed in sand.

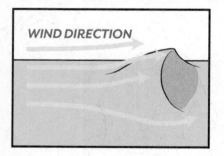

WIND DIRECTION

A dune can continue to grow and even migrate! Sand dunes are known for their ability to move and engulf roads, trees and even entire forests. A dune's migration is caused by sand being lifted and blown up the **windward** side of the dune and back down the **leeward** side, also called the **slip face**, landing at the edge of the dune.

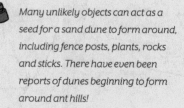

Many unlikely objects can act as a seed for a sand dune to form around, including fence posts, plants, rocks and sticks. There have even been reports of dunes beginning to form around ant hills!

Windward: the side that faces into the wind.
Leeward: the side that faces into the wind.
Slipface: also called the leeward side, the slipface may have got its name because of its steep angle, which can cause sand (and anything trying to walk on the dune) to slip down the slope!

Karst

Karst is a type of landscape made when acidic water seeps through cracks in the ground and slowly dissolves **limestone rock** over thousands or millions of years, leaving underground passages and spaces. Karst landscapes attract visitors and explorers, because caves, sinkholes and other interesting features can be found there.

It's a Cave Expedition!

Help the spelunker (or cave explorer) get through the cave maze to the main chamber!

START

FINISH

 Limestone is a rock that is made of tiny shells, corals, and skeletons of tiny ocean creatures. The limestone that is found on land was formed at the bottom of an ancient ocean!

Caves

A **cave** is a natural underground space that is large enough for people to fit inside. Caves are created through a variety of processes, including the weathering of rock, volcanic activity or landslides.

Label the Formations

There are many different formations in caves, including stalagmites, draperies and flowstone. Most are caused by the slow dripping of water, which over time deposits minerals. Draw a line from the cave formation terms to the correct drawing in the cave to the left.

DRAPERY: looks like stone curtains hanging from the ceiling.

STALACTITE: looks like an icicle made of stone.

COLUMN: these form when a stalactite and stalagmite meet.

STALAGMITE: these are usually thicker than stalactites.

FLOWSTONE: looks like a frozen waterfall.

*Memory Booster: stalag**mites** grow up from the ground and "**mite**" reach the ceiling, and stalac**tites** hold "**tite**" to the ceiling!*

Mountains

While there is no set definition of a **mountain**, most share certain characteristics: they are created by tectonic movement, they rise relatively quickly in elevation, have steeper sides than hills and have a defined peak, called a **summit**.

The Seven Summits are the highest peaks from each of the seven continents. Daring climbers challenge themselves to climb all seven mountains. Your challenge? Graph the towering heights of the Seven Summits!

The Seven Summits		
Everest	*Nepal/Tibet*	*29,029 ft*
Aconcagua	*Argentina*	*22,840 ft*
McKinley	*Alaska*	*20,320 ft*
Kilimanjaro	*Tanzania*	*19,339 ft*
Elbrus	*Russia*	*18,481 ft*
Vinson Massif	*Antarctica*	*16,067 ft*
Carstensz Pyramid	*Indonesia*	*16,023 ft*

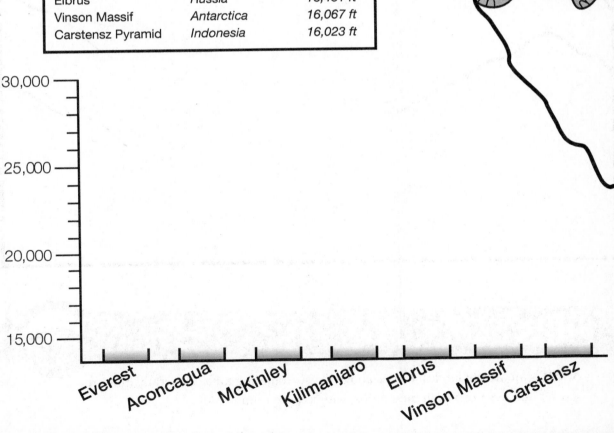

Valleys

A **valley** is the land between hills or mountains. They are formed by either water erosion from a river, or from ice erosion from a glacier. Throughout the ages, valleys have been popular areas for people to live because they usually have access to fresh water, are more protected from the elements, and have fertile soil.

Draw your own ancient valley city! Think about what ancient cities may have contained: is there a temple, or a palace? Is there a lake or a river, and where do the city inhabitants live?

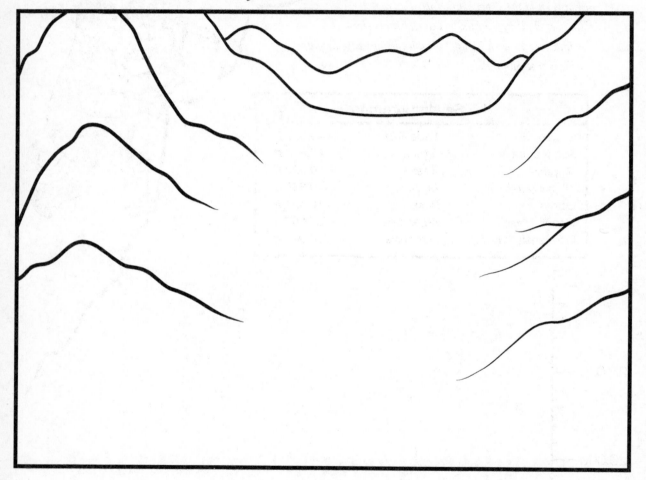

Hills

A **hill** is an area of land that rises above the surrounding area. Generally hills are shorter and less steep than mountains, with a more rounded top.

Peninsulas

A **peninsula** is a body of land that extends from a mainland into an ocean, sea, or lake. Peninsulas are usually surrounded on three sides by water.

Peninsula Match Up!

Match each famous peninsula with the correct name below.

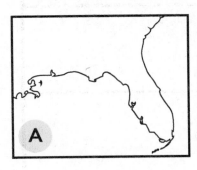

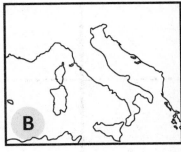

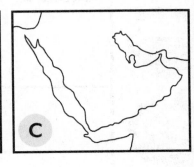

_____ Italian Peninsula   _____ Arabian Peninsula   _____ Florida Peninsula

Capes

A **cape** is a narrow point of land that juts into the ocean or other body of water. They are normally much smaller than peninsulas.

 Before 1914, ships that needed to get from the Atlantic ocean to the Pacific ocean had to sail around Cape Horn, at the southern tip of South America. That meant people and cargo going from New York to San Francisco traveled 13,000 miles! In 1914, after almost 35 years, the Panama Canal was completed, and it crossed the Panama Isthmus. This shortcut took 8,000 miles off of the New York to San Francisco trip.

Landform Recall!

You've read a lot about landforms so far! Use your new knowledge and test your memory by filling in the table below. For each icon found somewhere in this book, write the name of that landform and how it was created.

NAME	CAUSE

Unscramble Terms

Unscramble the landform vocabulary below. Then, write the correct definition for each term.

SITMUM: __ __ __ __ __ __

Definition: _____

_____

SETILATACT: __ __ __ __ __ __ __ __ __ __

Definition: _____

_____

SOUGINE: __ __ __ __ __ __ __

Definition: _____

_____

NELOIMEST: __ __ __ __ __ __ __ __ __

Definition: _____

_____

MITESTAGLA: __ __ __ __ __ __ __ __ __ __

Definition: _____

_____

DIMERYSENTA: __ __ __ __ __ __ __ __ __ __ __

Definition: _____

_____

MANDFLOR: __ __ __ __ __ __ __ __

Definition: _____

_____

HORMEPTAMIC: __ __ __ __ __ __ __ __ __ __ __

Definition: _____

_____

What do you think?

Erosion and weathering are usually caused by natural processes, but human activities also have a major impact on the amount of erosion that occurs. Can you think of ways that people move or alter land, and why people might want to do this?

_____

_____

_____

_____

_____

_____

_____

_____

_____

_____

_____

_____

_____

Explore Erosion & Deposition

As you've read, water can be a powerful force in reshaping the earth and moving materials. In this activity, think about the following questions: How does water erosion happen, and how can it change what a landscape looks like? How can deposition reshape landscapes?

You Will Need:

- Dirt
- Small gravel
- Sand
- Deep baking dish or pan
- Book
- Pencil
- Paper cups

The Grand Canyon in Arizona.

Instructions:

1. Begin by layering the dirt, gravel and sand at one end of the the baking dish, and use your hand to smooth out the surface to make your land, making sure to keep one side of the dish empty.

2. Dip your fingers into the water, and slowly drip the water over your land. Keep dripping water until your land is wet. What do you see happening when water falls on the dry land?

3. Gently lift up the end of your dish that contains your land. Place a book under that side to hold it up at an angle.

4. Use the tip of a pencil to poke a very small hole in your cup, and holding it above your land, slowly pour water into the cup. What do you see happening to the land as the water soaks in and drains? What happens to both ends of your dish, and what happens to the water? Record your observations, and include a drawing of your landscape.

5. Add another book to make a steeper angle, and repeat. Again, record your observations, and include a drawing.

6. How did your landscape change? What new landforms were created at either end of the dish?

Erosion, Weathering & Water

Water causes a lot of erosion and weathering, but we know that not all water does the same thing: streams and rivers move steadily down to the ocean, where waves lap gently or pound roughly against the shore. Compared to that, water in ponds and lakes barely move. So how does the movement of water affect weathering and erosion?

You Will Need:

- Three clear plastic cups
- Three candy-coated chocolates (three different colors is best)
- Water

The ocean waves have worn a hole through this rock outcropping on this beach in California.

Instructions:

1. Start by filling two of the cups with water, leaving one cup empty.

2. Place one piece of candy in each cup.

3. Take just one of the cups with water in it, and gently swirl the water inside for about 15 seconds. Do not swirl the other two cups.

4. Repeat the 15 second swirling every 4 or 5 minutes for an hour, and record your observations, and note any changes you notice in all three cups. You can label which cup to swirl if you like, to make sure you swirl the same cup.

5. Based on your observations, which has more of an effect: moving water, or still water? Why do you think this is? How do you think this translates to landforms?

60

Great job!

_____

is an Education.com science superstar

GEOGRAPHY MATH

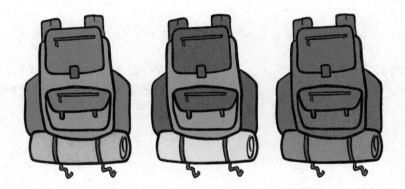

Reading Charts Practice I

Use the data found on the page "Mountains of the U.S."
and answer the questions below.

1 What is the name of the second highest mountain in California?

2 What is the name of the highest mountain in Alaska?

3 What is the name of the highest mountain in Colorado?

4 What is the name of the highest mountain in Washington?

5 In what state is the highest mountain in the United States that is not located in Alaska?

6 What is the name of the fifth highest mountain in Alaska?

7 What is the name of the third highest mountain in California?

8 What is the name of the tenth highest mountain in Colorado?

9 What is the name of the third highest mountain in Washington?

10 What is the name of the lowest mountain in Alaska that is listed on the chart?

Addition Problems

Use the data found on the page "Mountains of the U.S."
and answer the questions below.

use with
MOUNTAINS
chart

1 Add the heights of the highest mountains in Alaska and California.

2 Add the height of the highest mountain in Washington to the height of the second highest mountain in Washington.

3 Add the height of the third highest mountain in Colorado to the height of the fifth highest mountain in Alaska.

4 Add the height of the second highest mountain in Colorado to the height of the fourth highest mountain in California.

5 Add the height of the lowest mountain in Alaska to the height of the highest mountain in Colorado.

6 Add the heights of the lowest mountains in Washington and California.

7 Add the height of the lowest mountain in Colorado to the height of the third highest mountain in California.

8 Add the height of the fifth highest mountain in Alaska to the height of the third highest mountain in Washington.

Subtraction Problems

Use the data found on the page "Mountains of the U.S."
and answer the questions below.

1 Subtract the height of the highest mountain in California from the height of the highest mountain in Alaska.

2 Subtract the height of the second highest mountain in Washington from the height of the highest mountain in Washington.

3 Subtract the height of the third highest mountain in Colorado from the height of the fifth highest mountain in Alaska.

4 Subtract the height of the fourth highest mountain in California from the height of the second highest mountain in Colorado.

5 Subtract the height of the lowest mountain in Alaska from the height of the highest mountain in Colorado.

6 Subtract the height of the lowest mountain in California from the height of the lowest mountain in Washington.

7 Subtract the height of the lowest mountain in Colorado from the height of the third highest mountain in California.

8 Subtract the height of the third highest mountain in Washington from the height of the fifth highest mountain in Alaska.

Mixed Problems

Use the data found on the page "Mountains of the U.S."
and answer the questions below.

use with
MOUNTAINS
chart

1 How many mountains located in Washington are on the chart?

2 Subtract the lowest mountain from the highest mountain listed on the chart.

3 Subtract the height of Huron Peak in Colorado from the height of Mt Augusta in Alaska.

4 How many mountains located in California are on the chart?

5 Add the second lowest mountain listed on the chart and the second highest mountain listed.

6 Add the height of Mt. Yale in Colorado to the height of Mt. Whitney in California.

7 Add together the height of the three mountains located in Washington.

8 How many mountains on the chart are over 15,000 feet in height?

9 Subtract the height of Liberty Cap in Washington from the height of White Mountain in California.

10 Add the height of Castle Peak in Colorado to the height of Mt. Bear in Alaska.

Reading Charts Practice II

use with
ELEVATIONS
chart

Use the data found on the page "Elevations of the U.S."
and answer the questions below.

1 What state on the chart has the lowest point?

2 The highest point in one state is 11,239. Which state is this?

3 What state is Mt. Sunflower in?

4 How high is Backbone Mountain?

5 How many states have highest places under 1,000 feet?

6 What state is Boundary Peak in?

7 How high is Borah Peak?

8 How many states have highest points over 10,000 feet?

9 Which is higher, the highest place in Arkansas or the highest place in Minnesota?

10 Which is lower, the highest place in Maine or the highest place in New York?

Addition and Subtraction Problems

use with ELEVATIONS chart

Use the data found on the page "Elevations of the U.S."
and answer the questions below.

1 Subtract the height of the highest point in Arkansas from the height of the highest point in California.

2 Add the height of the highest point in Wyoming to the height of the highest point in North Carolina.

3 Subtract the height of the highest point in Georgia from the height of the highest point in Arizona.

4 Add the height of the highest points in Iowa and Tennessee.

5 Subtract the height of the highest point in Oregon from the height of the highest point in Montana.

6 Add the heights of the highest points in Louisiana and Connecticut.

7 Subtract the height of the highest point in North Dakota from the height of the highest point in South Dakota.

8 Add the heights of the highest points in New Jersey, Mississippi and Louisiana.

9 Add the height of the highest points in Rhode Island and Wisconsin. Then, subtract this amount from the height of the highest point in West Virginia.

10 Add the height of the highest points in Kansas and Kentucky. Then, subtract this amount from the height of the highest point in Colorado.

Easier Word Problems: To The Top

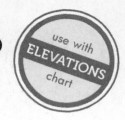
use with ELEVATIONS chart

Use the data found on the page "Elevations of the U.S."
and answer the questions below.

1 Jeannie and Rebecca climbed to the top of the highest points in North Carolina and South Carolina in the same week. How many feet did they climb to get to the top?

2 Jeannie and Rebecca climbed to the top of the highest point in Nebraska. Next, they climbed to the highest point in Kansas. How many more feet did they climb in Nebraska than in Kansas?

3 When Jeannie and Rebecca climbed up to the highest places in Mississippi, Louisiana and Alabama, how many feet did they climb in total?

4 Jeannie and Rebecca climbed to the top of the highest point in Wyoming. Next, they climbed the highest point in Montana. How many more feet did they climb in Wyoming than in Montana?

More Challenging Word Problems

use with
ELEVATIONS
chart

When you climb up to the top of a mountain, you have to climb down too! Use the data found on the page "Elevations of the U.S." and answer the questions below.

1 Jack and Simon climbed to the top of the highest point in Alaska, Mt. McKinley (which is also the highest mountain in all of the United States). Since they had to climb down Mt. McKinley as well, how many feet did they climb, up and down?

2 Jack and Simon climbed to the top of the highest point in New Mexico, where a helicopter picked them up and flew them to the highest point in Colorado. From there they made their descent. How many feet did they climb on the two mountains?

3 Jack and Simon climbed to the top of the highest point in New Hampshire, where a helicopter picked them up. The helicopter flew them to the bottom of the highest point in Maine, where they hiked to the top and back down. How many feet did they climb on the two mountains?

4 The highest point in Idaho is much higher than the highest point in Minnesota. Jack and Simon climbed up and down the highest point in Minnesota two times because they liked the scenery so much. How many more feet did they climb just to get to the top of the highest point in Idaho than they hiked in total in Minnesota?

Math Problem Basics: Dividing by 2

use with RIVERS chart

Use the data found on the page "Rivers of the U.S."
and answer the questions below.

When you measure the length of something, like a piece of rope, to find out what half of its length is, divide by 2.

For example: If a river is 422 miles long, half the length of the river is 211 feet long. 422 divided by 2 = 211.

1 How many miles is half of the Cumberland River?

2 How many miles is half of the Illinois River?

3 Add the lengths of the Little Missouri River and the Osage River. How many miles is half of this amount?

4 Add the lengths of the Ohio-Allegheny River and the Pecos River. How many miles is half of this amount?

5 How many miles is half of the Red River?

6 How many miles is half of the Salmon River added to the length of the Porcupine River?

7 How many miles is half of the Snake River added to half of the Smoky Hill River?

8 Add half the length of the Wabash River to half the length of the James River to the full length of the Powder River. How many miles did you get?

Math Problem Basics: Dividing by 3

use with RIVERS chart

Use the data found on the page "Rivers of the U.S."
and answer the questions below.

When you measure the length of something, like a piece of rope, to find out what one-third of that length is, all you have to do is divide by 3.

For example: If a river is 963 miles long, one-third of the length of the river is 321 feet long: 963 divided by 3 = 321.

1 How many miles is half of the Delaware River?

2 How many miles is one-third of the length of the Delaware River?

3 How many miles is one-third of the Canadian River?

4 How many miles is two-thirds of the Canadian River?

5 Add one-third of the Snake River to the length of the Washita River.

6 Add one-third of the Cumberland River to one-third of the North Platte River.

7 Add one-third of the Smoky Hill River to one-third of the Pend Oreille-Clark Fork River.

8 Subtract one-third of the Platte River from the length of the Ohio River.

Easier Word Problems

use with
RIVERS
chart

Use the data found on the page "Rivers of the U.S."
and answer the questions below.

1 Jim and Sam kayaked the entire length of the Rio Grande River. How many miles did they kayak?

2 Jim and Sam decided they wanted to kayak on two different rivers. Jim kayaked the entire length of the Roanoke River, and Sam kayaked the entire length of the Sacramento River. How many miles did the two friends kayak in total?

3 Jim and Sam decided they wanted to kayak on two different rivers. Jim kayaked the entire length of the Roanoke River, and Sam kayaked the entire length of the Sacramento River. How many more miles did Jim kayak than Sam?

4 Jim and Sam set out to kayak the entire length of the Snake River. Unfortunately, exactly half way through the trip Sam got sick and had to stop. Jim kept on kayaking until he reached the end. How many miles did Jim and Sam kayak on the Snake River in total?

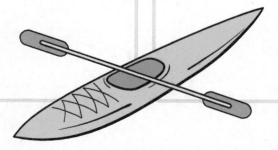

More Challenging Word Problems

use with
RIVERS
chart

Use the data found on the page "Rivers of the U.S."
and answer the questions below.

1 Sylvia and June canoed down the Pecos River. Exactly half way through, they had to stop because the rapids got too difficult. How many miles did the two friends canoe down the Pecos River?

2 Sylvia and June decided they wanted to canoe down the whole length of the Cimarron River. Exactly half way through, June's canoe sprung a leak, and she had to stop. Sylvia continued on all the way to the end. When she came to the end, she turned around and went back to pick up June. June got in Sylvia's canoe, and the two of them canoed all the way to the beginning of the river. How many miles did Sylvia canoe on the river?

3 Sylvia and June decided they wanted to canoe down two different rivers. Sylvia canoed down the Platte River, and June canoed down the North Platte River. Both of them had to stop exactly half way down the two rivers. How many more miles did Sylvia canoe than her friend June?

4 Sylvia and June wanted to canoe the full length of the Delaware River. Unfortunately, Sylvia had to stop after going one-third of the way down the river after her canoe sprung a leak. June got further, but she could only make it exactly half way down the river because of a dangerous lightning storm. How many miles in total did the two friends canoe down the Delaware River?

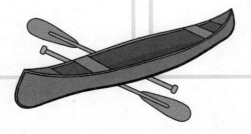

Atlantic Ocean Coastline

Use the data found on the page "Shorelines of the U.S."
and answer the questions below.

use with
SHORELINES
chart

1 Ava and her family live in the far north of North Carolina, and her uncle and his family live in the far south of South Carolina. When Ava's family visits her uncle, they drive the entire length of both coastlines. How many miles of coastline do Ava and her family travel to get to her uncle's house?

2 Mike lives in the southern-most city of Florida. Mike is a football player, and his high school team has to travel north to another Florida town to play their high school football team. The Florida coastline is 580 miles long. If the second Florida town is located on the coast 290 miles north of Mike's city, how much further does he have to travel to get to the Georgia coast?

3 Traveling the length of the Maine coastline takes eight hours. Traveling the length of the New Hampshire coastline takes only one hour. How long does it take to travel from the most northern city on the Maine coast to the southern most city on the New Hampshire coast? If you traveled 200 miles south from the northern most Maine city, how many more miles would you have to travel before you came to the New Hampshire border?

Gulf of Mexico Coastline

Use the data found on the page "Shorelines of the U.S."
and answer the questions below.

1 Travis lives on the Gulf Coast in the southern most city in Texas. His is visiting his friend Mindy, who lives hours away up the Texas coast. His starts his trip with a half tank of gas, so he has to get gas before he reaches Mindy's house. He stops to get gas 190 miles from his house. After he gets gas, he drives another 45 miles before he gets to Mindy's house. How many miles away from Travis's house is Mindy's house?

2 Jim lives at exactly the half-way point on the Gulf Coast of Florida, which is 385 miles from the northern most point of the coast. From his house, how many miles does Jim have to drive to get to the southern most point of the Florida coast?

3 Sandy and her family live at exactly the half-way point of the Mississippi Gulf Coast. The half-way point is 22 miles from both the Louisiana border and the Alabama border. Sandy loves a restaurant that is located on the Gulf Coast exactly on the border of Alabama and Florida. How many miles do Sandy and her family have to drive to get to the restaurant?

Pacific Ocean Coastline

Use the data found on the page "Shorelines of the U.S."
and answer the questions below.

use with
SHORELINES
chart

1 The distance between the northern most city on the Oregon coast and the southern most tip of California is 1,136 miles. Buster signed up for a sightseeing tour of the Oregon coast. The tour bus takes the passengers down the entire length of the Oregon coast. The California coast is 840 miles, so how many miles do Buster and the other tour passengers travel during their tour?

2 Sam lives in Canada. He is taking a vacation in Mexico, and he decides he wants to drive down the entire length of the Pacific Coast of the United States to get there. How many miles down the Pacific Coast will he travel before he reaches Mexico?

3 Julie is a marine biologist who works at an American college located on the Pacific Coast at the southern most tip of California. A group of seals she is studying live exactly at the border of the states Oregon and Washington. She knows that the coast line of California is 840 miles long. How many miles does she have to drive, if she leaves from her college, to get to the seals?

78

Mountains of the U.S.

use with MOUNTAINS worksheets

Name	State	Ht.	Name	State	Ht.	Name	State	Ht.
Mt. McKinley	AK	20,320	Castle Peak	CO	14,265	Windom Peak	CO	14,082
Mt. St. Elias	AK	18,008	Quandary Peak	CO	14,265	Mt. Columbia	CO	14,073
Mt. Foraker	AK	17,400	Mt. Evans	CO	14,264	Mt. Augusta	AK	14,070
Mt. Bona	AK	16,500	Longs Peak	CO	14,255	Missouri Mtn.	CO	14,067
Mt. Blackburn	AK	16,390	Mt. Wilson	CO	14,246	Humboldt Peak	CO	14,064
Mt. Sanford	AK	16,237	White Mtn.	CA	14,246	Mt. Bierstadt	CO	14,060
Mt. Vancouver	AK	15,979	North Palisade	CA	14,242	Sunlight Peak	CO	14,059
South Buttress	AK	15,885	Mt. Cameron	CO	14,238	Split Mtn.	CA	14,058
Mt. Churchill	AK	15,638	Mt. Shavano	CO	14,229	Handies Peak	CO	14,048
Mt. Fairweather	AK	15,300	Crestone Needle	CO	14,197	Culebra Peak	CO	14,047
Mt. Hubbard	AK	14,950	Mt. Belford	CO	14,197	Mt. Lindsey	CO	14,042
Mt. Bear	AK	14,831	Mt. Princeton	CO	14,197	Ellingwood Point	CO	14,042
East Buttress	AK	14,730	Mt. Yale	CO	14,196	Middle Palisade	CA	14,040
Mt. Hunter	AK	14,573	Mt. Bross	CO	14,172	Little Bear Peak	CO	14,037
Browne Tower	AK	14,530	Kit Carson Mtn.	CO	14,165	Mt. Sherman	CO	14,036
Mt. Alverstone	AK	14,500	Mt. Wrangell	AK	14,163	Redcloud Peak	CO	14,034
Mt. Whitney	CA	14,494	Mt. Sill	CA	14,162	Mt. Langley	CA	14,027
University Peak	AK	14,470	Mt. Shasta	CA	14,162	Conundrum Peak	CO	14,022
Mt. Elbert	CO	14,440	El Diente Peak	CO	14,159	Mt. Tyndall	CA	14,019
Mt. Massive	CO	14,421	Point Success	WA	14,158	Pyramid Peak	CO	14,018
Mt. Harvard	CO	14,420	Maroon Peak	CO	14,156	Wilson Peak	CO	14,017
Mt. Rainier	WA	14,410	Tabeguache Mtn.	CO	14,155	Wetterhorn Peak	CO	14,015
Mt. Williamson	CA	14,370	Mt. Oxford	CO	14,153	North Maroon Peak	CO	14,014
La Plata Peak	CO	14,361	Mt. Sneffels	CO	14,150	San Luis Peak	CO	14,014
Blanca Peak	CO	14,345	Mt. Democrat	CO	14,148	Middle Palisade	CA	14,012
Uncompahgre Peak	CO	14,309	Capitol Peak	CO	14,130	Mt. Muir	CA	14,012
Crestone Peak	CO	14,294	Liberty Cap	WA	14,112	Mt. of the Holy Cross	CO	14,005
Mt. Lincoln	CO	14,286	Pikes Peak	CO	14,110	Huron Peak	CO	14,003
Grays Peak	CO	14,270	Snowmass Mtn.	CO	14,092	Thunderbolt Peak	CA	14,003
Mt. Antero	CO	14,269	Mt. Russell	CA	14,088	Sunshine Peak	CO	14,001
Torreys Peak	CO	14,267	Mt. Eolus	CO	14,083			

Elevations of the U.S.

use with
ELEVATIONS
worksheets

State	Highest point	Elev (ft.)
Alabama	Cheaha Mountain	2,405
Alaska	Mt. McKinley	20,320
Arizona	Humphreys Peak	12,633
Arkansas	Mount Magazine	2,753
California	Mt. Whitney	14,494
Colorado	Mt. Elbert	14,440
Connecticut	Mt. Frissell	2,380
Delaware	Ebright Road	448
D.C.	Tenleytown	410
Florida	Britton Hill	345
Georgia	Brasstown	4,784
Hawaii	Puu Wekiu	13,796
Idaho	Borah Peak	12,662
Illinois	Charles Mound	1,235
Indiana	Hoosier Hill	1,257
Iowa	Hawkeye Point	1,670
Kansas	Mt. Sunflower	4,039
Kentucky	Black Mountain	4,145
Louisiana	Driskill Mountain	535
Maine	Mt. Katahdin	5,267
Maryland	Backbone Mountain	3,360
Massachusetts	Mt. Greylock	3,491
Michigan	Mt. Arvon	1,979
Minnesota	Eagle Mountain	2,301
Mississippi	Woodall Mountain	806
Missouri	Taum Sauk Mountain	1,772
Montana	Granite Peak	12,799

State	Highest point	Elev (ft.)
Nebraska	Panorama Point	5,424
Nevada	Boundary Peak	13,140
New Hampshire	Mt. Washington	6,288
New Jersey	High Point	1,803
New Mexico	Wheeler Peak	13,167
New York	Mt. Marcy	5,344
North Carolina	Mt. Mitchell	6,684
North Dakota	White Butte	3,506
Ohio	Campbell Hill	1,549
Oklahoma	Black Mesa	4,973
Oregon	Mt. Hood	11,239
Pennsylvania	Mt. Davis	3,213
Rhode Island	Jerimoth Hill	812
South Carolina	Sassafras Mountain	3,560
South Dakota	Harney Peak	7,242
Tennessee	Clingmans Dome	6,643
Texas	Guadalupe Peak	8,751
Utah	Kings Peak	13,528
Vermont	Mt. Mansfield	4,393
Virginia	Mt. Rogers	5,729
Washington	Mt. Rainier	14,410
West Virginia	Spruce Knob	4,863
Wisconsin	Timms Hill	1,951
Wyoming	Gannett Peak	13,804
United States	**Mt. McKinley (AK)**	**20,320**

Rivers of the U.S.

River	Length
Alabama-Coosa	600 mi
Altamaha-Ocmulgee	392 mi
Apalachicola-Chattahoochee	524 mi
Arkansas	1,459 mi
Brazos	923 mi
Canadian	906 mi
Cimarron	600 mi
Colorado	1,450 mi
Colorado	862 mi
Columbia	1,243 mi
Colville	350 mi
Connecticut	407 mi
Cumberland	720 mi
Delaware	390 mi
Gila	649 mi
Green	360 mi
Green	730 mi
Illinois	420 mi
James/Dakota	710 mi
Kanawha-New	352 mi
Kansas	743 mi
Koyukuk	470 mi
Kuskokwim	724 mi
Licking	350 mi
Little Missouri	560 mi
Milk	625 mi
Mississippi	2,348 mi
Mississippi-Missouri-Red Rock	3,710 mi

River	Length
Missouri	2,315 mi
Missouri-Red Rock	2,540 mi
Mobile-Alabama-Coosa	645 mi
Neosho	460 mi
Niobrara	431 mi
Noatak	350 mi
North Canadian	800 mi
North Platte	618 mi
Ohio	981 mi
Ohio-Allegheny	1,306 mi
Osage	500 mi
Ouachita	605 mi
Pearl	411 mi
Pecos	926 mi
Pee Dee-Yadkin	435 mi
Pend Oreille–Clark Fork	531 mi
Platte	990 mi
Porcupine	569 mi
Potomac	383 mi
Powder	375 mi
Red	1,290 mi
Red River of the North	545 mi
Republican	445 mi
Rio Grande	1,900 mi
Roanoke	380 mi
Sabine	380 mi
Sacramento	377 mi
Saint Francis	425 mi

River	Length
Salmon	420 mi
San Joaquin	350 mi
San Juan	360 mi
Santee-Wateree-Catawba	538 mi
Smoky Hill	540 mi
Snake	1,038 mi
South Platte	424 mi
Stikine	379 mi
Susquehanna	444 mi
Tanana	659 mi
Tennessee	652 mi
Tennessee—French Broad	886 mi
Tombigbee	525 mi
Trinity	360 mi
Wabash	512 mi
Washita	500 mi
White	722 mi
Wisconsin	430 mi
Yellowstone	692 mi
Yukon	1,979 mi

Shorelines of the U.S.

use with SHORELINES worksheets

State	General Coastline (miles)	Tidal Shoreline (miles)
Atlantic Coast:		
Maine	228	3,478
New Hampshire	13	131
Massachusetts	192	1,519
Rhode Island	40	384
Connecticut	—	618
New York	127	1,850
New Jersey	130	1,792
Pennsylvania	—	89
Delaware	28	381
Maryland	31	3,190
Virginia	112	3,315
North Carolina	301	3,375
South Carolina	187	2,876
Georgia	100	2,344
Florida (Atlantic)	580	3,331
Total Atlantic Coast	**2,069**	**28,673**

State	General Coastline (miles)	Tidal Shoreline (miles)
Gulf Coast:		
Florida (Gulf)	770	5,095
Alabama	53	607
Mississippi	44	359
Louisiana	397	7,721
Texas	367	3,359
Total Gulf Coast	**1,631**	**17,141**

	General Coastline (miles)	Tidal Shoreline (miles)
Pacific Coast:		
California	840	3,427
Oregon	296	1,410
Washington	157	3,026
Hawaii	750	1,052
Alaska (Pacific)	5,580	31,383
Total Pacific Coast	**7,623**	**40,298**

	General Coastline (miles)	Tidal Shoreline (miles)
Arctic Coast:		
Alaska (Arctic)	1,060	2,521
Total Arctic Coast	**1,060**	**2,521**

	General Coastline (miles)	Tidal Shoreline (miles)
COAST TOTAL	**12,383**	**88,633**

Great job!

_____

is an Education.com math superstar

ANSWERS

Why is the sky blue?

To understand why the sky is blue, we must first understand the physics of light and color.

The light from the sun seems white to us, but white light is actually made up of all the colors of the spectrum: red, orange, yellow, green, blue, indigo and violet!

We see objects in color because those objects absorb some of the colors in white light, and reflect the colors that we see! For example, grass reflects the color green and absorbs all the other colors.

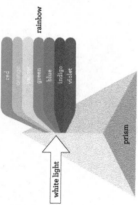

white light

prism

red
orange
yellow
green
blue
indigo
violet

rainbow

The sky is blue because it has to travel through Earth's atmosphere, where there are lots of gases that absorb red, orange and yellow colors. Then, the blue light gets scattered all across the sky, which is what we see when we look into the sky.

QUESTION & ANSWER:

What colors make up the white light of the sun?

It is made up of all the colors of the spectrum like red, orange, yellow, green, blue, indigo and violet.

If you see a blue car, what color/s does it reflect?

The blue car reflects the color blue.

If you see a red apple, what color/s does it absorb?

The red apple would absorb all the colors of the spectrum except the color red.

page 2

Why is the ocean blue?

red
orange
yellow
green
blue
indigo
violet

blue is reflected

All the other colors are absorbed.

The ocean appears blue to us because of the light from the sun.

We often think that the sun's light just allows us to see, but without light, colors wouldn't even exist!

What we see as white light from the sun is actually a combination of all the colors of the rainbow. Try and imagine red, orange, yellow, green, blue, indigo and violet rays of light streaming from the sun. Objects either absorb or reflect these rays.

When the sun's light hits the ocean, the red, orange, yellow, green, indigo and violet rays are absorbed so that we can't see them! Only the blue light is reflected. The ocean itself isn't really blue; we're just seeing the reflected blue light.

QUESTION & ANSWER:

What colors make up the light from the sun?

It is a combination of all the colors of the rainbow: red, orange, yellow, green, blue, indigo and violet.

What color/s does the ocean reflect?

The ocean reflects the color blue.

What color/s does the ocean absorb?

The ocean absorbs all the colors of the rainbow, except the color blue.

page 3

Why do people blush?

When some people get embarrassed, their cheeks turn red. We call this blushing, and it also can occur when a person is anxious or angry.

The science behind blushing is pretty simple: your body sends extra blood to your face which causes your cheeks to redden. The reason this happens is not so clear. Scientists have suggested that our bodies blush to reveal how we really feel. Next time you're anxious to get in a game or embarrassed that you dropped your ice cream on the floor, your cheeks just might give you away!

Did you know that some people are afraid of blushing? The fear of blushing is called erythrophobia.

Why do you think people suffer from erythrophobia?

QUESTION & ANSWER:

What causes your cheeks to redden?
It is when the body sends excess blood to your face.

What is a possible reason behind blushing?
Blushing occurs when a person is anxious or angry.

What is erythrophobia?
It is the fear of blushing.

Why do we hiccup?

The often annoying hiccup happens when our diaphragms get upset.

The diaphragm is a muscle at the bottom of the rib cage that helps pull air into our lungs when we breathe. Every once in a while, the diaphragm gets irritated and starts pulling air into the lungs the wrong way. We experience this as a hiccup.

Eating too quickly, drinking cold beverages, and swallowing air are just a handful of ways the diaphragm can get upset enough to cause hiccups. In other words, the diaphragm can be kind of sensitive.

There are lots of "home remedies" that people use to get rid of the hiccups. Lots of them are silly.

Do you think any of these methods actually work? Why or why not?

Eat a spoonful of sugar.

Drink water from the opposite side of the glass.

Chug a glass of water.

Hold your breath.

Get SCARED!

Cover your ears.

What methods do you use to cure your hiccups?

QUESTION & ANSWER:

Hiccups are caused by the involuntary contraction of what muscle?
diaphragm

Write down some ways that the diaphragm can be irritated.
eating too quickly, drinking cold beverages and swallowing air

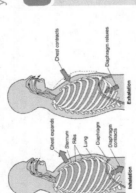

WHY AND HOW

Why do cats purr?

Cats purr for the same reason that humans sigh, smile and sing. It's a communication tool that means different things at different times.

A cat's purr can be broken down into three separate categories: the happy purr, the friendly purr and the reassuring purr.

The happy purr is the most popular purr. When you scratch a cat behind the ears, the purr signals the cat's own comfort and enjoyment. The friendly purr often happens when a cat is approached by a human he likes or another cat. This second type of purr simply communicates that the cat welcomes the visitor. Lastly, cats use the reassuring purr when they are afraid. Scientists believe that purring calms the cat, in the same way humans sometimes sing when they're nervous to make them feel better.

Mechanics behind a purr:

Purrs involve various muscles in a cat's body. The larynx, or voice box, and diaphragm play key roles in the mechanics of purring.

vocal cords

The diaphragm moves the air in and out of the vibrating vocal cords which causes the sound.

Identification:

Based on the reading, identify what type of purr cats make in these situations:

happy purr .... a cat being scratched

friendly purr .... two cats walking towards each other

reassuring purr .... a cat at a vet

happy purr .... when a cat gets a treat

reassuring purr .... a mother cat giving birth

reassuring purr .... when approached by a stranger

WHY AND HOW

Why does ice float?

Even though ice is the solid form of water, it actually has a lower density than its liquid counterpart.

When water freezes, its molecules actually spread out a bit and organize themselves into crystal arrangements. Water molecules, on the other hand, have tightly packed molecules. So when you put an ice cube into a glass of water, the ice cannot sink to the bottom of the glass because the molecules in the water are too dense.

cold water molecules

ice molecules

ACTIVITY:

Try your own experiment. You know that ice cubes float in water, but what about other liquids? Record your findings here.

.... Olive Oil

.... Vegetable Oil

.... Nail Polish

.... Oil Paint

.... Maple Syrup

Why does the earth spin?

The Earth spins because there is nothing in its way to stop it!

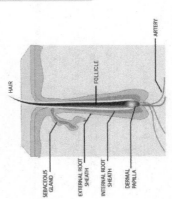

Long before our planet was a solid sphere, there was just a mass of dust and gas. Earth was formed when all this matter began to spin. That's how most planets and stars are formed!

Thousands of years later, the spinning cloud of dust and gas became our planet, and thanks to our position in the Solar System, neither the sun nor the moon had the power to slow Earth's rotation enough to halt it completely.

Imagine the Earth did not spin. How would this affect your life?

★ Remember that the Earth's rotation is responsible for the sun rising and setting. If the Earth did not spin, parts of our planet would spend half a year in darkness and another half a year in full sunlight.

QUESTION & ANSWER:

What was Earth before it became a solid sphere?
A mass of dust and gas

How was Earth formed?
It was formed from the spinning cloud of dust and gas.

Can the sun and the moon stop Earth from spinning?
No

Why does hair turn gray?

To find out why hair turns gray we have to investigate *hair follicles*.

Hair follicles are tubes of tissue that surround the roots of each hair strand. Inside the hair follicles are *pigment cells* that determine if our hair is red, brown, black or blond. As people age, their hair follicles start to die. Without enough pigment cells from these dying hair follicles, hair gradually turns gray or white.

QUESTION & ANSWER:

What are the tubes of tissue that surround the roots of each hair strand?
Hair Follicles

Located inside the hair follicles, what determines the color of our hair?
Pigment Cells

What helps determine whether a person's hair turns gray or white?
Genes

There isn't a certain age when every person starts getting gray hair. It depends on each individual's *genes*. A good way to predict when or if someone you know might get gray hair is to look at that person's parents or grandparents.

HAIR
FOLLICLE
ARTERY
SEBACEOUS GLAND
EXTERNAL ROOT SHEATH
INTERNAL ROOT SHEATH
DERMAL PAPILLA

90

Why is there a leap year?

The month of February usually has 28 days, but every four years it has 29. To understand this we have to understand what a year is.

One year is supposed to match the time it takes for the Earth to orbit the Sun. However, the match isn't perfect. Our year equals 365 days, but it takes Earth about 365 ¼ days to complete its orbit. That little fraction may seem insignificant, but every four years it adds up to a complete day. We give that extra day to February and call it leap year.

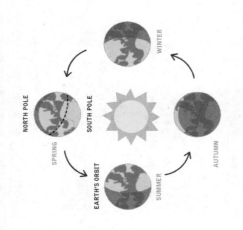

NORTH POLE
SOUTH POLE
SPRING
EARTH'S ORBIT
WINTER
SUMMER
AUTUMN

Why is it called leap year when we're actually adding a day? It seems like it might make more sense to call it some thing like plus day or add day. We call it leap year because the addition of that one day effectively leaps the rest of that year forward by 24 hours.

A "leap year baby" is someone who is born on the last day of February in a leap year. Would a leap year baby age differently than everyone else?

QUESTION & ANSWER:

How long does it take the Earth to complete its orbit?
It takes the Earth 365 ¼ days to complete its orbit.

How often does a leap year occur?
A leap year occurs every 4 years.

What is a person born on February 29 th called?
A leap year baby

A leap year consists of how many days?
It consists of 366 days as opposed to a regular 365 days.

How is honey made?

Without bees we wouldn't have any delicious honey to sweeten our toast or tea. Honey bees work tirelessly to produce honey in a multi-step process that is both wonderful and a bit disgusting.

First, honey bees have to use their tongues to slurp out the pollen and nectar from flowers. They actually digest all of this, allowing the pollen and nectar to mix with the proteins and enzymes of their stomachs. When the honey bees return to their hive, they regurgitate–a fancy word for throwing up this pollen/nectar/protein /enzyme mix into a beeswax comb.

The bees then flap their wings to help the mixture thicken before covering the combs with a wax cap.

After beekeepers take out these honeycombs, all they need to do is process and clean out the combs a bit. The odd combination of flower parts and bee proteins is now honey!

Can you help our bee friend find his mate?

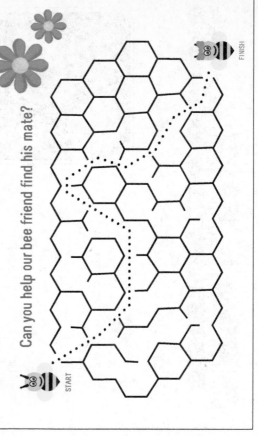

START
FINISH

How is a pearl formed?

Have you ever had a small piece of dust get in your eye? It was probably annoying, but when an oyster gets dust inside its shell, it turns the dust speck into a pearl!

Oysters try and protect themselves from unwanted visitors by covering any outside dust particles with a mineral substance called nacre. Layers and layers of nacre eventually form a pearl.

Natural pearls form when a piece of dust gets into an oyster's shell by chance. Cultured pearls are the result of humans forcing a dust particle into an oyster's shell. Pearls are so popular today that a lot of people don't want to wait for a pearl to form naturally!

Can you think of anything else in nature that starts off small and plain, but after a long time turns into something beautiful?

QUESTION & ANSWER:

How do oysters protect themselves?
They protect themselves by covering any outside dust particles with a mineral substance called nacre.

How do natural pearls form?
They form when a piece of dust gets into an oyster's shell by chance.

How do cultured pearls form?
They form when humans force a dust particle into an oyster's shell.

How is a star born?

A star is a big ball of plasma that is formed from a cloud of dust and gas.

Sometimes particles of dust and gas float by each other in space without anything happening. Other times gravity clumps these clouds together into compact substances. The particles begin bouncing off of each other, creating friction and heat. Eventually, the heat becomes so intense that it creates a nuclear reaction which releases a massive amount of energy and light. The resulting substance is a star.

Did you know that celebrities and actors are often called stars? Why do you think we compare famous people to burning lights in the sky?

QUESTION & ANSWER:

What is a star?
It is a big ball of plasma that is formed from a cloud of dust and gas.

What gets released after a nuclear reaction involving intense heat?
A massive amount of energy and light gets released.

ENERGY IS ALL AROUND US

Humans have always depended on energy for many things. From basic survival, such as cooking food, to the luxuries of television and video games, energy is an important part of our daily lives.

Before electricity, humans had to rely on the other sources of energy found in nature to complete tasks.

ACTIVITY

Look at the pictures below and label what form of energy is being used.

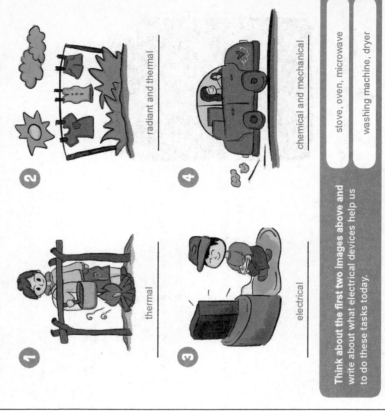

1. thermal

2. radiant and thermal

3. electrical

4. chemical and mechanical

Think about the first two images above and write about what electrical devices help us to do these tasks today.

stove, oven, microwave

washing machine, dryer

page 25

POTENTIAL VERSUS KINETIC ENERGY

Take a look at the chart to see some examples of potential and kinetic energy.

POTENTIAL ENERGY	KINETIC ENERGY
A car sitting in the driveway	A car driving down the street
A ball in a basketball player's hands	A ball bouncing down the court
A sleeping child	A child jumping on the bed
A log in a fireplace	A burning log
A lamp	A lamp turned on

Look at the pictures below, and label them potential or kinetic based on what type of energy they are showing.

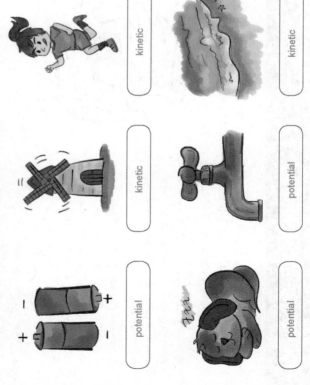

kinetic

kinetic

kinetic

potential

potential

potential

page 23

92

WHAT IS WIND ENERGY?

Wind is caused by convection currents (flow of air) in Earth's atmosphere. The sun produces the heat energy that produces these currents. The wind is full of kinetic energy.

Wind can be transferred into electrical energy with the help of wind turbines. A **turbine** is a machine powered by rotating blades.

The blades of a wind turbine move when there is wind. The energy is then transferred to a generator by a spinning shaft.

Windmills work the same as turbines. They are used for grinding grains or pumping water. These have been used around the world for over 1000 years.

Wind must be blowing at a rate of at least 14 miles per hour to power a turbine or windmill. Very strong winds, however, can damage these structures.

THINK AND RESPOND

What are the pros and cons of building wind turbines in Florida?

Hint: Think about the location of this state and what type of weather affects the area.

Think and respond answers will vary but should

include a pro about the ocean breeze and a con

about potential hurricanes.

_____

_____

WHAT IS BIOMASS ENERGY?

Biomass fuels come from living things such as trees, plants and crop residue. As long as we continue to grow trees and plants and replace those we use by planting new ones, we will always have biomass fuels.

TAKE A LOOK AT HOW BIOMASS ENERGY IS PRODUCED.

1 The original source of biomass fuels is from the sun. The energy is stored in trees and plants.

2 When trees or plants die or are cut down, they are burned.

3 Steam is released and moves blades inside a turbine or generator.

4 The power is then transferred to homes and businesses via cables.

power cables

★ THINK AND RESPOND ★

1. List 5 reasons why people cut down trees.

Answer will vary.

2. Why is it important that we plant new trees?

Answer will vary but you may include: trees are needed for many things including energy

so it is important to replace what we use.

WHAT IS GEO-THERMAL ENERGY?

Geo-Thermal energy is produced by hot rocks underground. To harness this energy, deep wells are drilled into the Earth. Then, cold water is pumped down into these wells. When the water goes through cracks in the rock, it is heated up. Upon its return to the surface, it has transformed into steam and hot water. This energy is then used to power generators.

Most places on the planet where geo-thermal energy is found are not visible. However, there are some places where geo-thermal energy makes its way to the surface. These places are volcanoes, fumaroles, hot springs and geysers.

A VOLCANO is a vent in the Earth's crust where hot, melted rock comes out.

A FUMAROLE is a hole in the ground where vapors and gas come out. These are usually found in volcanic regions.

A HOT SPRING is a source of water which flows out at a temperature higher than the average temperature of other springs.

A GEYSER is a spring that occasionally shoots out hot water and steam.

Using the vocabulary above (words in purple), complete the following sentences.

1. There is a ___geyser___ in Yellowstone National Park named Old Faithful that shoots out hot water several times a day.

2. When a ___volcano___ is erupting, it is a good idea to get out of its path.

3. Many people take advantage of the warm waters of a ___hot spring___.

4. The steam coming out of a ___fumarole___ looks a lot like smoke.

WHAT IS WATER ENERGY?

Water energy, also known as hydro power, is generated by moving water. The kinetic energy in moving water can be transferred into electricity. Here's how electricity is made at a hydroelectric power plant.

STEP 1
A dam is built to collect water (usually on a large river).

STEP 2
A gate is opened in the dam to allow water to rush into a large pipe. The pipe is sloped so that the water moves quickly, creating large amounts of kinetic energy.

STEP 3
The rushing water moves blades, which in turn sends power to a generator.

★ THINK AND RESPOND ★

Could a hydroelectric power plant be built on a lake? Explain why or why not.

Yes, because a lake can be a large body of water.

94

NON-RENEWABLE ENERGY

FOSSIL FUELS

Most non-renewable energy is generated from fossil fuels which include coal, petroleum (crude oil) and natural gas. These are known as fossil fuels because of the way they are formed.

Fossil fuels were formed deep within the Earth from the remains of ancient animals and plants. Over a long period of time, heat and pressure turned these remains into fuel which releases energy when it is burned. Because they take millions of years to form, these fuels are considered non-renewable. If we run out of these, we will have to turn to alternative sources of energy.

COMPARE Using the Venn diagram, compare fossil fuels to solar energy.

FOSSIL FUELS   SOLAR ENERGY

Answers will vary

Answers will vary

RENEWABLE ENERGY
review

ANSWER THE FOLLOWING QUESTIONS ABOUT RENEWABLE ENERGY.

1. Why is it important to try to use as many renewable resources as possible?

It is important to use renewable resources because they'll always be available. Non-renewable energy sources, like fossil fuels, will eventually run out.

2. Name all 5 renewable energy sources and give a brief description of each.

Geo-thermal: This type of energy is produced by hot rocks deep beneath Earth's surface.

Wind: The wind's energy is converted to electricity through the use of turbines.

Biomass: This type of energy comes from living things like trees and plants.

Water: Hydro power is created by converting the energy of moving water into electricity.

Solar: This type of energy comes from the Sun.

LOOK AT THE FOLLOWING PICTURES AND LABEL THEM ACCORDING TO WHICH RENEWABLE ENERGY SOURCE THEY DEMONSTRATE.

geo-thermal   water   wind   solar   biomass

Answers and Solutions

Landforms Wordsearch

```
K C A N Y O N L B P M E S A
M P N B P C T A E U U H E U
R O D P L A T E A U T T Y
H R U D L V P K A R S T K A
J U V N E E A T J R H O E R
V I A K T K C L I F F A D
A S L E H A E I K I E D T A
L H C T I M I H A C T U X N
L A A U F A G N U R R N L G
E I P O A D E J R B I E W O
Y P E N I N S U L A S O Y F
S J A F A R A S E U H I L L
```

Find the following landform terms in the wordsearch.

Karst	Mountain	Plateau	Peninsula
Cave	Yardang	Canyon	Cape
Valley	Butte	Cliff	
Hill	Mesa	Dune	

page 42

VOCABULARY REVIEW

USE THE CLUES AND THE WORD BOX TO COMPLETE THE WORD SEARCH.

ENERGY	POTENTIAL	KINETIC	RENEWABLE	NON-RENEWABLE	BIOMASS
VOLCANO	FUMAROLE	GEYSER	HOT SPRING	SOLAR CELL	SOLAR PANEL
TURBINE	CONSERVE				

Tip: → ↓ → ↗ ↘ ↙

```
P V B I O M A S S C A G Q U U T O E P F
D O G X X P R E O J H U E U U Q L I A O
R L Z X G W O N L S R M W Y B Q H R T
T C W S R P S T O O M E D I A X C O J R
U A T A O E J L E R R K S W G F O T E C
R N S W R E A E A N T A E Y L J I S N J
B O Z V I R N R N T N M U E S G P E M
I G E O C I L I M E I M U N G L R R S
N P A E B G G M X R V A A O F E M I G G
E T L R S O L A R P A N E L O P S N Y U
N O N R E N E W A B L E M N O N Z G O D
L L E C R A L O S G W K I N E T I C L B
```

- Energy in motion is called ____kinetic____ energy.
- Stored energy is called ____potential____ energy.
- A machine powered by rotating blades is a ____turbine____.
- A spring that shoots out hot water is a ____geyser____.
- Sources of energy that will never run out are known as ____renewable____ energy.
- Energy that comes from things such as plants and trees is known as ____biomass____ energy.
- ____Energy____ is the ability to do work.
- A hole in the ground that has vapors or gases coming out is called a ____fumarole____.
- A tool that changes light energy into electricity is a ____solar cell____.
- ____Conserve____ means to use something in small amounts.
- A ____volcano____ is a vent in Earth's crust in which melted rock comes out.
- Energy available in a specific amount that will not regenerate is known as: ____non-renewable____ energy.
- A ____solar panel____ is a group of solar cells connected to form a large, flat surface.
- A source of warm water is called a ____hot spring____.

page 37

96

Answers and Solutions

Landscape Labeling!

1) <u>Plateau</u>
2) <u>Canyon</u>
3) <u>Mesa</u>
4) <u>Butte</u>

Answers and Solutions

Continental Match-up!

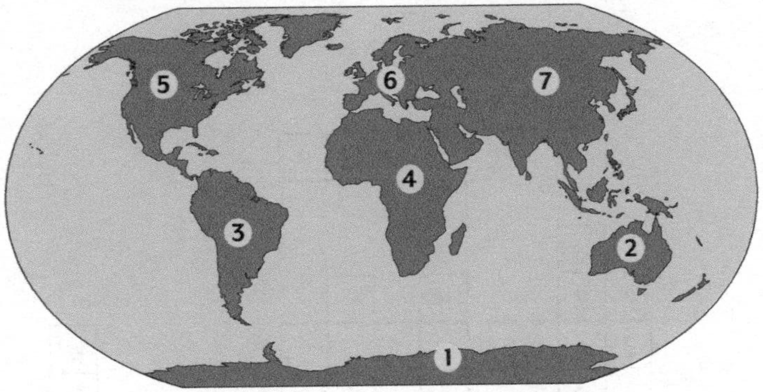

7 AASI <u>A S I A</u>
4 RIAFAC <u>A F R I C A</u>
1 ICARTACTAN <u>A N T A R C T I C A</u>
5 TRONH REICAMA <u>N O R T H   A M E R I C A</u>
6 REOPEU <u>E U R O P E</u>
3 SHOUT CERIAAM <u>S O U T H   A M E R I C A</u>
2 STAIURALA <u>A U S T R A L I A</u>

Answers and Solutions

Canyon Crossword

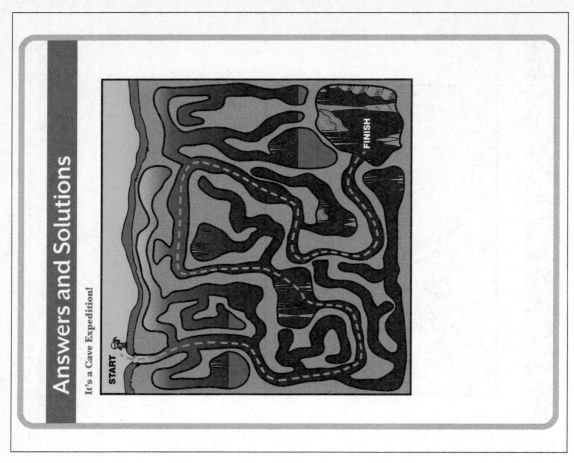

Answers and Solutions

It's a Cave Expedition!

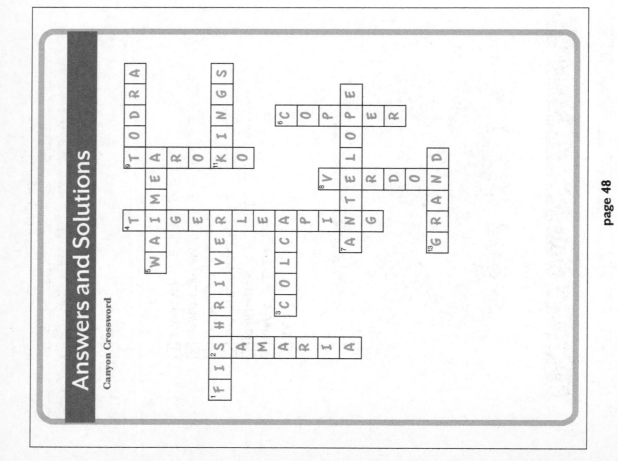

Answers and Solutions

Label the Formations

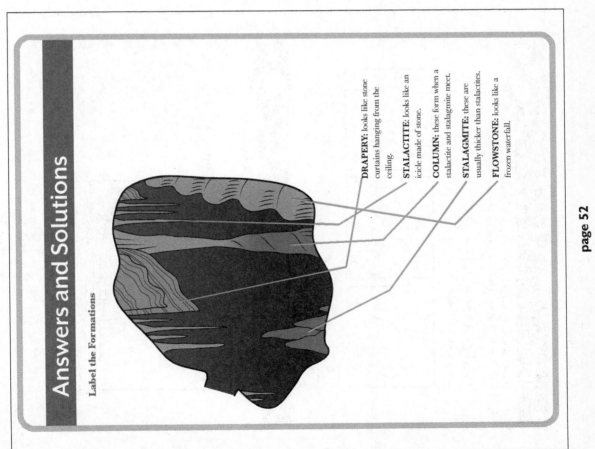

DRAPERY: looks like stone curtains hanging from the ceiling.

STALACTITE: looks like an icicle made of stone.

COLUMN: these form when a stalactite and stalagmite meet.

STALAGMITE: these are usually thicker than stalactites.

FLOWSTONE: looks like a frozen waterfall.

page 52

Answers and Solutions

Graph the Seven Summits

The Seven Summits		
Everest	Nepal/Tibet	29,029 ft
Aconcagua	Argentina	22,840 ft
McKinley	Alaska	20,320 ft
Kilimanjaro	Tanzania	19,339 ft
Elbrus	Russia	18,481 ft
Vinson Massif	Antarctica	16,067 ft
Carstensz Pyramid	Indonesia	16,023 ft

Bar graph with vertical axis marked 30,000 — 25,000 — 20,000 — 15,000 and horizontal categories: Everest, Aconcagua, McKinley, Kilimanjaro, Elbrus, Vinson Massif, Carstensz

page 53

Answers and Solutions

Landform Total Recall

NAME	CAUSE
Mesa	Mesas are worn down by weathering and erosion, caused by wind and water.
Mountain	Mountains are usually formed by tectonic uplift.
Cave	Caves are usually formed by the dissolving of limestone rock by water.
Dune	Dunes are formed from windblown sand in an arid location.
Valley	Valleys are usually formed by rivers or glaciers.
Canyon	Canyons are usually formed by rivers.
Karst	Karst landscapes are formed by the dissolving of limestone rock by water.

Peninsulas

A **peninsula** is a body of land that extends from a mainland into an ocean, sea, or lake. Peninsulas are usually surrounded on three sides by water.

Peninsula Match Up!

Match each famous peninsula with the correct name below.

B Italian Peninsula

C Arabian Peninsula

A Florida Peninsula

Capes

A **cape** is a narrow point of land that juts into the ocean or other body of water. They are normally much smaller than peninsulas.

Before 1914, ships that needed to get from the Atlantic ocean to the Pacific ocean had to sail around Cape Horn, at the southern tip of South America. That meant people and cargo going from New York to San Francisco traveled 13,000 miles! In 1914, after almost 35 years, the Panama Canal was completed, and it crossed the Panama Isthmus. This shortcut took 8,000 miles off of the New York to San Francisco trip.

ANSWERS
Reading Charts Practice I

Use the data found on the page "Mountains of the U.S." and answer the questions below.

1 What is the name of the second highest mountain in California?

Mt. Williamson

2 What is the name of the highest mountain in Alaska?

Mt. McKinley

3 What is the name of the highest mountain in Colorado?

Mt. Elbert

4 What is the name of the highest mountain in Washington?

Mt. Rainier

5 In what state is the highest mountain in the United States that is not located in Alaska?

California, Mt. Whitney

6 What is the name of the fifth highest mountain in Alaska?

Mt. Blackburn

7 What is the name of the third highest mountain in California?

White Mountain

8 What is the name of the tenth highest mountain in Colorado?

Mt. Antero

9 What is the name of the third highest mountain in Washington?

Liberty Cap

10 What is the name of the lowest mountain in Alaska that is listed on the chart?

Mt. Augusta

page 64

Answers and Solutions

Landform Unscramble

SITMUM: S U M M I T

Definition: The peak of a mountain.

SETILATACT: S T A L A C T I T E

Definition: A rock formation that hangs from the ceiling of a cave, that is caused by dripping water.

SOUGINE: I G N E O U S

Definition: Rock that has been formed from cooled and hardened lava.

NELOIMEST: L I M E S T O N E

Definition: Rock that was formed at the bottom of an ancient ocean, out of tiny fossils.

MITESTAGLA: S T A L A G M I T E

Definition: A rock formation that grows from the bottom of a cave, that is caused by dripping water.

DIMERYSENTA: S E D I M E N T A R Y

Definition: Rock that has been formed by compressed layers of sediment.

MANDFLOR: L A N D F O R M

Definition: Any natural feature of Earth's surface that is made of rock, dirt or minerals.

HORMEPTAMIC: M E T A M O R P H I C

Definition: Rock that was formed from sedimentary rock that has undergone heat and extreme pressure.

page 57

101

ANSWERS
Addition Problems

Use the data found on the page "Mountains of the U.S." and answer the questions below.

1 Add the heights of the highest mountains in Alaska and California.

Mt. McKinley   20,320
Mt. Whitney + 14,494
34,814

2 Add the height of the highest mountain in Washington to the height of the second highest mountain in Washington.

Mt. Rainier   14,410
Point Success + 14,158
28,568

3 Add the height of the third highest mountain in Colorado to the height of the fifth highest mountain in Alaska.

Mt. Harvard   14,420
Mt. Blackburn + 16,390
30,810

4 Add the height of the second highest mountain in Colorado to the height of the fifth highest mountain in California.

Mt. Massive   14,421
Mt. Sill   + 14,162
28,583

5 Add the height of the lowest mountain in Alaska to the height of the highest mountain in Colorado.

Mt. Augusta   14,070
Mt. Elbert + 14,440
28,510

6 Add the heights of the lowest mountains in Washington and California.

Liberty Cap   14,112
Thunderbolt Peak + 14,003
28,115

7 Add the height of the lowest mountain in Colorado to the height of the third highest mountain in California.

Sunshine Peak   14,001
White Mtn.   + 14,246
28,247

8 Add the height of the fifth highest mountain in Alaska to the height of the third highest mountain in Washington.

Mt. Blackburn   16,390
Liberty Cap   + 14,112
30,502

ANSWERS
Subtraction Problems

Use the data found on the page "Mountains of the U.S." and answer the questions below.

1 Subtract the height of the highest mountain in California from the height of the highest mountain in Alaska.

Mt. McKinley   20,320
Mt. Whitney - 14,494
5,826

2 Subtract the height of the second highest mountain in Washington from the height of the highest mountain in Washington.

Mt. Rainier   14,410
Point Success - 14,158
252

3 Subtract the height of the third highest mountain in Colorado from the height of the fifth highest mountain in Alaska.

Mt. Blackburn   16,390
Mt. Harvard - 14,420
1,970

4 Subtract the height of the fourth highest mountain in California from the height of the second highest mountain in Colorado.

Mt. Massive   14,421
North Palisade - 14,242
179

5 Subtract the height of the lowest mountain in Alaska from the height of the highest mountain in Colorado.

Mt. Elbert   14,440
Mt. Augusta - 14,070
370

6 Subtract the height of the lowest mountain in California from the height of the lowest mountain in Washington.

Liberty Cap   14,112
Thunderbolt Peak - 14,003
109

7 Subtract the height of the lowest mountain in Colorado from the height of the third highest mountain in California.

White Mtn.   14,246
Sunshine Peak - 14,001
245

8 Subtract the height of the third highest mountain in Washington from the height of the fifth highest mountain in Alaska.

Mt. Blackburn   16,390
Liberty Cap   - 14,112
2,278

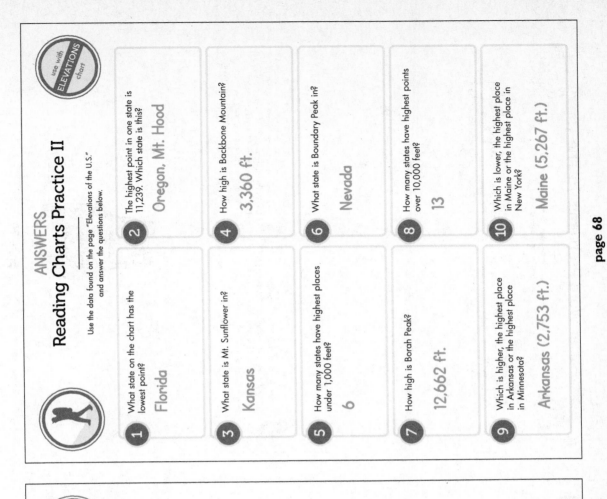

Reading Charts Practice II

Use the data found on the page "Elevations of the U.S." and answer the questions below.

1 What state on the chart has the lowest point?

Florida

2 The highest point in one state is 11,239. Which state is this?

Oregon, Mt. Hood

3 What state is Mt. Sunflower in?

Kansas

4 How high is Backbone Mountain?

3,360 ft.

5 How many states have highest places under 1,000 feet?

6

6 What state is Boundary Peak in?

Nevada

7 How high is Borah Peak?

12,662 ft.

8 How many states have highest points over 10,000 feet?

13

9 Which is higher, the highest place in Arkansas or the highest place in Minnesota?

Arkansas (2,753 ft.)

10 Which is lower, the highest place in Maine or the highest place in New York?

Maine (5,267 ft.)

page 68

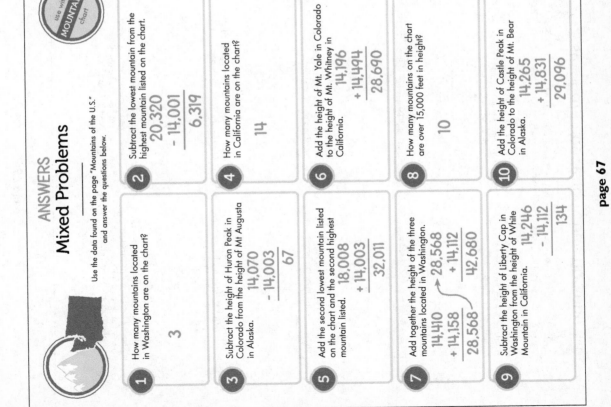

Mixed Problems

Use the data found on the page "Mountains of the U.S." and answer the questions below.

1 How many mountains located in Washington are on the chart?

3

2 Subtract the lowest mountain from the highest mountain listed on the chart.

20,320
− 14,001
  6,319

3 Subtract the height of Huron Peak in Colorado from the height of Mt Augusta in Alaska.

14,070
− 14,003
     67

4 How many mountains located in California are on the chart?

14

5 Add the second lowest mountain listed on the chart and the second highest mountain listed.

18,008
+ 14,003
32,011

6 Add the height of Mt. Yale in Colorado to the height of Mt. Whitney in California.

14,196
+ 14,494
28,690

7 Add together the height of the three mountains located in Washington.

14,410 → 28,568
14,158   + 14,112
28,568   42,680

8 How many mountains on the chart are over 15,000 feet in height?

10

9 Subtract the height of Liberty Cap in Washington from the height of White Mountain in California.

14,246
− 14,112
     134

10 Add the height of Castle Peak in Colorado to the height of Mt. Bear in Alaska.

14,265
+ 14,831
29,096

page 67

103

Addition and Subtraction Problems

use with ELEVATIONS *chart*

Use the data found on the page "Elevations of the U.S."
and answer the questions below.

1 Subtract the height of the highest point in Arkansas from the height of the highest point in California.

```
  14,494
-  2,753
  11,741
```

2 Add the height of the highest point in Wyoming to the height of the highest point in North Carolina.

```
  13,804
+  6,684
  20,488
```

3 Subtract the height of the highest point in Georgia from the height of the highest point in Arizona.

```
  12,633
-  4,784
   7,849
```

4 Add the height of the highest points in Iowa and Tennessee.

```
   1,670
+  6,643
   8,313
```

5 Subtract the height of the highest point in Oregon from the height of the highest point in Montana.

```
  12,799
- 11,239
   1,560
```

6 Add the heights of the highest points in Louisiana and Connecticut.

```
    535
+ 2,380
  2,915
```

7 Subtract the height of the highest point in North Dakota from the height of the highest point in South Dakota.

```
   7,242
-  3,506
   3,736
```

8 Add the heights of the highest points in New Jersey, Mississippi and Louisiana.

```
  1,803      2,609
+   806     +  535
  2,609      3,144
```

9 Add the height of the highest points in Rhode Island and Wisconsin. Then, subtract this amount from the height of the highest point in West Virginia.

```
    812      4,863
+ 1,951    - 2,763
  2,763      2,100
```

10 Add the height of the highest points in Kansas and Kentucky. Then, subtract this amount from the height of the highest point in Colorado.

```
  4,039     14,440
+ 4,145    - 8,184
  8,184      6,256
```

Easier Word Problems: To The Top

use with ELEVATIONS *chart*

Use the data found on the page "Elevations of the U.S."
and answer the questions below.

1 Jeannie and Rebecca climbed to the top of the highest points in North Carolina and South Carolina in the same week. How many feet did they climb to get to the top?

```
   6,684
+  3,560
  10,244
```

2 Jeannie and Rebecca climbed to the top of the highest point in Nebraska. Next, they climbed to the highest point in Kansas. How much higher did they climb in Nebraska than in Kansas?

```
   5,424
-  4,039
   1,385
```

3 When Jeannie and Rebecca climbed up to the highest places in Mississippi, Louisiana and Alabama, how many feet did they climb in total?

```
    806
    535
+ 2,405
  3,746
```

4 Jeannie and Rebecca climbed to the top of the highest point in Wyoming. Next, they climbed the highest point in Montana. How many more feet did they climb to get to the top in Wyoming than in Montana?

```
  13,804
- 12,799
   1,005
```

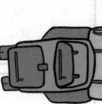

ANSWERS
Math Problem Basics: Dividing by 2

Use the data found on the page "Rivers of the U.S." and answer the questions below.

When you measure the length of something, like a piece of rope, to find out what half of its length is, divide by 2.

For example: If a river is 422 miles long, half the length of the river is 211 feet long. 422 divided by 2 = 211.

1 How many miles is half of the Cumberland River?

720 ÷ 2 = 360

2 How many miles is half of the Illinois River?

420 ÷ 2 = 210

3 Add the lengths of the Little Missouri River and the Osage River. How many miles is half of this amount?

560 + 500 = 1,060
1060 ÷ 2 = 530

4 Add the lengths of the Ohio-Allegheny River and the Pecos River. How many miles is half of this amount?

1306 + 926 = 2,232
2,232 ÷ 2 = 1,116

5 How many miles is half of the Red River?

1,290 ÷ 2 = 645

6 How many miles is half of the Salmon River added to the length of the Porcupine River?

420 ÷ 2 = 210
210 + 569 = 779

7 How many miles is half of the Snake River added to half of the Smoky Hill River?

1,038 ÷ 2 = 519
540 ÷ 2 = 270
519 + 270 = 789

8 Add half the length of the Wabash River to half the length of the James River to the full length of the Powder River. How many miles did you get?

512 ÷ 2 = 256
710 ÷ 2 = 355

256
355
+ 375
986

ANSWERS
More Challenging Word Problems

When you climb up to the top of a mountain, you have to climb down too! Use the data found on the page "Elevations of the U.S." and answer the questions below.

1 Jack and Simon climbed to the top of the highest point in Alaska, Mt. McKinley (which is also the highest mountain in all of the United States). Since they had to climb down Mt. McKinley as well, how many feet did they climb, up and down?

20,320
× 2
40,640

OR

20,320
+ 20,320
40,640

2 Jack and Simon climbed to the top of the highest point in New Mexico, where a helicopter picked them up and flew them to the highest point in Colorado. From there they made their descent. How many feet did they climb on the two mountains?

NM   CO

14,440
+ 13,167
27,607

3 Jack and Simon climbed to the top of the highest point in New Hampshire, where a helicopter picked them up. The helicopter flew them to the bottom of the highest point in Maine, where they hiked to the top and back down. How many feet did they climb on the two mountains?

NH

5,267
× 2
10,534

ME

10,534
+ 6,288
16,822

4 The highest point in Idaho is much higher than the highest point in Minnesota. Jack and Simon climbed up and down the highest point in Minnesota two times because they liked the scenery so much. How many more feet did they climb just to get to the top of the highest point in Idaho than they hiked in total in Minnesota?

2,301
× 4
9,204

12,662
− 9,204
3,458

Easier Word Problems

Use the data found on the page "Rivers of the U.S."
and answer the questions below.

1 Jim and Sam kayaked the entire length of the Rio Grande River. How many miles did they kayak?

1,900 miles

2 Jim and Sam decided they wanted to kayak on two different rivers. Jim kayaked the entire length of the Roanoke River, and Sam kayaked the entire length of the Sacramento River. How many miles did the two friends kayak in total?

$$\begin{array}{r} 380 \\ + 377 \\ \hline 757 \end{array}$$

3 Jim and Sam decided they wanted to kayak on two different rivers. Jim kayaked the entire length of the Roanoke River, and Sam kayaked the entire length of the Sacramento River. How many more miles did Jim kayak than Sam?

$$\begin{array}{r} 380 \\ - 377 \\ \hline 3 \end{array}$$

4 Jim and Sam set out to kayak the entire length of the Snake River. Unfortunately, exactly half way through the trip Sam got sick and had to stop. Jim kept on kayaking until he reached the end. How many miles did Jim and Sam kayak on the Snake River in total?

$1,038 \div 2 = 519$
$519 + 1,038 = 1,557$

Math Problem Basics: Dividing by 3

Use the data found on the page "Rivers of the U.S."
and answer the questions below.

When you measure the length of something, like a piece of rope, to find out what one-third of that length is, all you have to do is divide by 3.

For example: If a river is 963 miles long, one-third of the length of the river is 321 feet long: 963 divided by 3 = 321.

1 How many miles is half of the Delaware River?

$390 \div 2 = 195$

2 How many miles is one-third of the length of the Delaware River?

$390 \div 3 = 130$

3 How many miles is one-third of the Canadian River?

$906 \div 3 = 302$

4 How many miles is two-thirds of the Canadian River?

$906 \div 3 = 302$
$302 + 302 = 604$

5 Add one-third of the Snake River to the length of the Washita River.

$1,038 \div 3 = 346$
$346 + 500 = 846$

6 Add one-third of the Cumberland River to one-third of the North Platte River.

$720 \div 3 = 240$
$618 \div 3 = 206$
$240 + 206 = 446$

7 Add one-third of the Smoky Hill River to one-third of the Pend Oreille-Clark Fork River.

$540 \div 3 = 180$
$531 \div 3 = 177$
$180 + 177 = 357$

8 Subtract one-third of the Platte River from the length of the Ohio River.

$990 \div 3 = 330$
$981 - 330 = 651$

More Challenging Word Problems

Use the data found on the page "Rivers of the U.S." and answer the questions below.

1 Sylvia and June canoed down the Pecos River. Exactly half way through, they had to stop because the rapids got too difficult. How many miles did the two friends canoe down the Pecos River?

926 ÷ 2 = 463

2 Sylvia and June decided they wanted to canoe down the whole length of the Cimarron River. Exactly half way through, June's canoe sprung a leak, and she had to stop. Sylvia continued on all the way to the end. When she came to the end, she turned around and went back to pick up June. June got in Sylvia's canoe, and the two of them canoed all the way to the beginning of the river. How many miles did Sylvia canoe on the river?

600 × 2 = 1,200

3 Sylvia and June decided they wanted to canoe down two different rivers. Sylvia canoed down the Platte River, and June canoed down the North Platte River. Both of them had to stop exactly half way down the two rivers. How many more miles did Sylvia canoe than her friend June?

990 ÷ 2 = 495
618 ÷ 2 = 309
495 - 309 = 186

4 Sylvia and June wanted to canoe the full length of the Delaware River. Unfortunately, Sylvia had to stop after going one-third of the way down the river after her canoe sprung a leak. June got further, but she could only make it exactly half way down the river because of a dangerous lightning storm. How many miles in total did the two friends canoe down the Delaware River?

390 ÷ 3 = 130
390 ÷ 2 = 195
130 + 195 = 325

Atlantic Ocean Coastline

Use the data found on the page "Shorelines of the U.S." and answer the questions below.

1 Ava and her family live in the far north of North Carolina, and her uncle and his family live in the far south of South Carolina. When Ava's family visits her uncle, they drive the entire length of both coastlines. How many miles of coastline do Ava and her family travel to get to her uncle's house?

301
+ 187
488

2 Mike lives in the southern-most city of Florida. Mike is a football player, and his high school team has to travel north to another Florida town to play their high school football team. The Florida coastline is 580 miles long. If the second Florida town is located on the coastline 290 miles north of Mike's city, how much further does he have to travel to get to the Georgia coastline?

580
- 290
290

3 Traveling the length of the Maine coastline takes eight hours. Traveling the length of the New Hampshire coastline takes only one hour. How long does it take to travel from the most northern city on the Maine coastline to the southern most city on the New Hampshire coastline? If you traveled 200 miles south from the northern most Maine city, how many more miles would you have to travel before you came to the New Hampshire border?

8 hours + 1 hour = 9 hours

228 - 200 = 28

ANSWERS
Pacific Ocean Coastline

Use the data found on the page "Shorelines of the U.S." and answer the questions below.

1 The distance between the northern most city on the Oregon coast and the southern most tip of California is 1,136 miles. Buster signed up for a sightseeing tour of the Oregon coast. The tour bus takes the passengers down the entire length of the Oregon coast. The California coast is 840 miles, so how many miles do Buster and the other tour passengers travel during their tour?

$$\begin{array}{r} 1,136 \\ -\ 840 \\ \hline 296 \end{array}$$

2 Sam lives in Canada. He is taking a vacation in Mexico, and he decides he wants to drive down the entire length of the Pacific Coast of the United States to get there. How many miles down the Pacific Coast will he travel before he reaches Mexico?

$$\begin{array}{r} 157 \\ 296 \\ +\ 840 \\ \hline 1,293 \end{array}$$

3 Julie is a marine biologist who works at an American college located on the Pacific Coast at the southern most tip of California. A group of seals she is studying live exactly at the border of the states Oregon and Washington. She knows that the coast line of California is 840 miles long. How many miles does she have to drive, if she leaves from her college, to get to the seals?

$$\begin{array}{r} 296 \\ +\ 840 \\ \hline 1,136 \end{array}$$

page 78

ANSWERS
Gulf of Mexico Coastline

Use the data found on the page "Shorelines of the U.S." and answer the questions below.

1 Travis lives on the Gulf Coast in the southern most city in Texas. He is visiting his friend Mindy, who lives hours away up the Texas coast. He starts his trip with a half tank of gas, so he has to get gas before he reaches Mindy's house. He stops to get gas 190 miles from his house. After he gets gas, he drives another 45 miles before he gets to Mindy's house. How many miles away from Travis's house is Mindy's house?

$$\begin{array}{r} 190 \\ +\ 45 \\ \hline 235 \end{array}$$

2 Jim lives at exactly the half-way point on the Gulf Coast of Florida, which is 385 miles from the northern most point of the coast. From his house, how many miles does Jim have to drive to get to the southern most point of the Florida coast?

$$\begin{array}{r} 770 \\ -\ 385 \\ \hline 385 \end{array}$$

3 Sandy and her family live at exactly the half-way point of the Mississippi Gulf Coast. The half-way point is 22 miles from both the Louisiana border and the Alabama border. Sandy loves a restaurant that is located on the Gulf Coast exactly on the border of Alabama and Florida. How many miles does Sandy and her family have to drive to get to the restaurant?

$$\begin{array}{r} 22 \\ +\ 53 \\ \hline 75 \end{array}$$

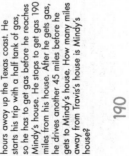

page 77

108